Heinemann is an imprint of Pearson Education Limited,
a company incorporated in England and Wales, having
its registered office at Edinburgh Gate, Harlow, Essex, CM20 2JE.
Registered company number: 872828

Heinemann is a registered trademark of Pearson Education Limited

First published in *The Drama Library* 1960

First published in *The Hereford Plays Series* 1963

First published in the *Heinemann Plays* series 1996

19

ISBN:978 0 435233 20 4

Designed by Jeffrey White Creative Associates

Typeset by Books Unlimited (Nottm) NG19 7QZ

Cover photo © Getty

Cover design by Clare Webber

Printed in China (CTPS/19)

CONTENTS

PREFACE

In this edition of *A Man for All Seasons*, you will find notes, questions and activities to help in studying the play in class, particularly at GCSE level.

The introduction provides background information on the author and the social context of the play. It outlines the story, discusses performance and examines the characters in detail.

The activities at the end of the book range from straightforward *Keeping Track* questions which can be tackled at the end of each act to focus close attention on what is happening in the play, to more detailed work on character, performance, themes and criticism in the *Explorations* section.

There is also a bibliography detailing other works by Bolt, as well as critical studies.

If you are already using the Hereford edition of *A Man for All Seasons*, you will find that the page numbering in the actual playscript is the same, allowing the two editions to be easily used side by side.

INTRODUCTION

Robert Bolt

Robert Bolt was born in Manchester in 1924, the son of a furniture dealer. He was educated at Manchester Grammar School, from where he went to work in an insurance office. During World War II he served in the Royal Air Force and in the Royal West Africa Frontier Force. After the end of the war he studied history at Manchester University; he then trained to teach at Exeter University. As a schoolmaster, he worked at Millfield public school in Somerset.

It was during this time as a teacher that Bolt took up playwriting, first for the radio and then for the stage. His first commercially presented play, *The Critic and the Heart*, was presented at the Oxford Playhouse in 1957; in the same year he achieved his first success in London with *Flowering Cherry*. As a result he was able to give up teaching in order to write full time. In 1960 he had two plays produced in London, *The Tiger and the Horse* and, in July, *A Man for All Seasons*: both of these plays focused upon the demands and responsibilities of commitment, both personal and political, as a major theme.

At this time, Bolt, previously a member of the Communist Party, was sentenced to one month's imprisonment for refusing to renounce civil disobedience in protesting against nuclear weapons for the Campaign for Nuclear Disarmament. On his release, he started work on the first of several film screenplays, *Lawrence of Arabia* (about T. E. Lawrence) for the director David Lean; this was later followed by the script for Lean's *Doctor Zhivago*, for both of which Bolt won Oscars. Bolt also continued to write for the theatre: *Gentle Jack* was staged in 1963, *The Thwarting of Baron Bolligrew* (a play for children) in 1965 and *Vivat! Vivat Regina*, in which the major characters are Queen Elizabeth I and Mary, Queen of Scots, in 1970. In 1977 his play *State of Revolution*, a version of the events before and after the Russian revolution, was presented at the National Theatre in London.

Further screenplays included *Ryan's Daughter* (1970), *The Bounty* (with Mel Gibson and Antony Hopkins in 1984) and *The Mission* (1986). In

1983, however, he underwent heart by-pass surgery and then suffered a stroke which left him paralysed on his right side. He continued to work nevertheless, principally on adaptations and screenplays for both film and television. He died in February 1995, aged 70.

A Man for All Seasons remains his best known and most appreciated stage play. In common with much of his work, it dramatizes historical events and characters in order to explore the demands of duty, responsibility and commitment and their effects upon the individual. It received a mixed critical reception on its opening in 1960, but became a great success with the public, running for 320 performances. This led, in turn, to its being filmed in 1967, with Paul Scofield recreating the part of Sir Thomas More which he had created on the stage. For this screenplay Bolt also won an Oscar. The play continues to be produced and seen worldwide.

The theatrical context

In the 1950s the Berliner Ensemble theatre company, led by the German writer and director Bertolt Brecht, had visited London with several productions. Their style of presentation, which became known as 'Brechtian', was strongly influential in the English theatre of the late 1950s and early 1960s. Bolt employs many Brechtian devices in *A Man for All Seasons*.

Generally, English theatre at this time was naturalistic: the action of plays was presented in a realistic, naturalistic way in settings that were as realistic and naturalistic as possible. In short, the aim of theatrical productions was to create and present as accurate an illusion of reality as possible to the audience. The Brechtian approach to theatre was the reverse of this: through the use of various 'alienation effects', the audience were reminded throughout that they were sitting in a theatre, watching an artificial creation. This, in turn, was intended to encourage them to judge the actions of the characters and the contents of the plays. The audience was not merely being entertained: it was taking part in the theatrical event and was encouraged to create dramatic meaning for itself.

Bolt borrows various Brechtian alienation effects in *A Man for All Seasons*: direct address to the audience, to set the scene and introduce characters, is given to the Common Man, who also assumes a variety of roles throughout the play. At one point, the Common Man reads from a history book, telling the audience of the fates of the characters in the play whom they are at that moment watching. The set is intended to remain the same throughout, with various screens and flats flown on and off stage merely to suggest new settings as appropriate, all executed in full view of the audience. These and other lesser effects all reinforce to the audience that they are watching a theatrical version of events that took place over a number of years. They also allow the story to be told flexibly and economically, enabling the audience to remain engaged in the events of the play as they develop and as More's dilemma resolves itself. Finally, they allow the Common Man to deliver what appears to be the 'moral' of the play: 'if you must make trouble, make the sort of trouble that's expected.'

The historical context

As has already been noted, the action of the play actually took place over several years: More was appointed Lord Chancellor in 1530, and he died in 1535. The historical events which form the background to the action of the play are as follows.

After the Wars of the Roses, Henry VII became King of England in 1485. He had two sons, Arthur and Henry. Naturally it was expected that Arthur, the first son, would in his turn become King, so in order to secure the new Tudor dynasty Arthur was married to Catherine of Aragon from Spain, thus allying England with the major European power of the time. It was not foreseen that Arthur would die young, before becoming King, thus creating possible future instability and losing the Spanish alliance.

It was decided, therefore, that Arthur's younger brother Henry, who was now the heir to the throne, should marry the widowed Catherine of Aragon. While the teachings of the Catholic church forbade a man to marry his brother's widow, a dispensation to allow this was granted by the Pope, based on the book of Deuteronomy (chapter 25, verse 17) of the Old Testament of the Bible. Hence, when Henry died in 1509, Henry VIII became King with Catherine as his queen.

Their marriage, however, produced no sons who survived infancy: Henry became increasingly desperate for a male heir. Furthermore, in the book of Leviticus in the Old Testament Henry read that any man who married his brother's wife would be punished by being unable to produce a male heir. Henry became disenchanted with Catherine and convinced that he was being punished for his sin in marrying her. At the same time he fell in love with Anne Boleyn. The solution he decreed was to secure a divorce from Catherine, but this could only be achieved by another dispensation from the Pope in Rome. Rome was by now occupied by the Spanish King Charles V, who naturally sought to protect Catherine of Aragon. It appeared, therefore, that Henry was powerless.

At this time, dissatisfaction with the Catholic Church was growing across Europe. It was seen by some of its critics, including Martin Luther, to be increasingly corrupt and self-serving, exploiting its position as the only Christian church in Europe with the power even to overrule kings in their own countries. The Catholic Church's response to its critics was to expel or excommunicate them, which would lead, according to its teachings, to eternal damnation. Luther, among others, protested against this power and instigated the Reformation, establishing his own Protestant Christian Church.

Henry, being unable to secure the dispensation that he wanted to achieve his divorce, was able to take advantage of these developments. He broke with the Catholic Church in Rome, establishing his own Church of England, through which he was able to arrange the divorce for himself in his position as supreme Head of the Church in England. This position was guaranteed for the King by the Act of Supremacy, which effectively subordinated the Church to the powers of the State through the Head of State, the King.

It is More's position in these events which is the focus of *A Man for All Seasons*. When Wolsey, Henry's Chancellor, died in 1530, More became Chancellor. His loyalty as an individual, however, remained with the Roman Catholic Church, and the play follows the clash between Henry, determined on the divorce and absolute support from all his subjects in his policy, and More, determined to walk the tightrope between public agreement with Henry and private satisfaction of his conscience. This, of course, became impossible with the Act of Supremacy, so More resigned as Chancellor.

Finally, to guarantee absolute political support for his reforms, Henry introduced the Act of Succession to a Parliament unable and unwilling to do anything but agree. By the Act of Succession, it became law that children of the marriage between Henry and Anne Boleyn, whom he had married in 1533, were to be his heirs; in addition, all influential men were required to swear an oath supporting this act or they would face a charge of high treason, punishable by death. It was this oath that More refused to take, seeing it as further degradation of the principles in which he believed. As a result, he was arrested and subsequently executed. While Bolt of necessity presents a relatively simplified version of these events, in the trial scene he quotes More's words from the trial itself, with the result that Thomas More speaks across more than 400 years to a modern audience.

As a footnote to these events, it is worth noting that More, who was renowned in his lifetime for his knowledge, scholarship and integrity, was made a saint by the Catholic Church in 1935.

Reading the play

All plays are written to be performed or, at the very least, read aloud. In reading *A Man for All Seasons*, More's wit and intelligence, his wife Alice's forthright nature and his daughter Margaret's quick-witted character all become vivid; indeed, as the action of the play progresses, More's word-play becomes a major part of his defence. By contrast, in the speech of Wolsey and especially Cromwell, both of whom are professional politicians, considerable layers of subtext add depth to the surface meaning of what they say: both characters are, after all, solely concerned with doing the King's business. King Henry is presented as a youthful, vigorous and mercurial man, the sudden changes of mood clearly reflected in his speech. Of the other characters, the self-serving Richard Rich's rise is clearly reflected in his increasingly confident speech, while the strength of William Roper's principles is clearly reflected in the strength of his expression; the Spanish Ambassador Chapuys remains a constantly teasing diplomatic presence. The Common Man, who also functions as the narrator of the play while taking on a variety of small functional parts, stands alone as the only character who addresses the audience directly in a manner that is humorous, barbed and, finally, hard-headed.

The play is formally divided into two acts but, within each act, various scenes are easily identifiable; they are usually marked by narration or comment from the Common Man and a change of location. Hence, the various scenes of the play lend themselves to reading and rehearsing in groups. A useful approach is to read sections aloud first of all to understand the context and the action: then explore and experiment with the text to discover more depth and understanding of the characters, their actions and reactions and how they combine in order to further the development of the plot.

Following the play text you will find two series of questions entitled *Keeping Track* and *Explorations*. *Keeping Track* is intended to help your understanding of the characters and action of the play as it develops and can be used while reading the play for the first time. *Explorations* are more detailed and demanding questions organized according to the characters, themes, performance and criticism. The questions in this section may lead to coursework assignments or examination practice. All the questions are designed to stimulate knowledge, understanding and, hopefully, enjoyment of the play.

Tim Bezant

AUTHOR'S PREFACE

The bit of English History which is the background to this play is pretty well known. Henry VIII, who started with everything and squandered it all, who had the physical and mental fortitude to endure a lifetime of gratified greeds, the monstrous baby whom none dared gainsay, is one of the most popular figures in the whole procession. We recognise in him an archetype, one of the champions of our baser nature, and are in him vicariously indulged.

Against him stood the whole edifice of medieval religion, founded on piety, but by then as moneyed, elaborate, heaped high and inflexible as those abbey churches which Henry brought down with such a satisfying and disgraceful crash.

The collision came about like this: While yet a Prince, Henry did not expect to become a King, for he had an elder brother, Arthur. A marriage was made between this Arthur and a Spanish Princess, Catherine, but Arthur presently died. The Royal Houses of Spain and England wished to repair the connection, and the obvious way to do it was to marry the young widow to Henry, now heir in Arthur's place. But Spain and England were Christian Monarchies and Christian law forbade a man to marry his brother's widow.

To be a Christian was to be a Churchman and there was only one church (though plagued with many heresies) and the Pope was its head. At the request of Christian Spain and Christian England the Pope dispensed with the Christian law forbidding a man to marry his brother's widow, and when in due course Prince Henry ascended the English throne as Henry VIII, Catherine was his Queen.

For some years the marriage was successful; they respected and liked one another, and Henry took his pleasures elsewhere but lightly. However, at length he wished to divorce her.

The motives for such a wish are presumably as confused, inaccessible and helpless in a King as any other man, but here are three which make sense: Catherine had grown increasingly plain and intensely religious; Henry had fallen in love with Anne Boleyn; the Spanish alliance had become unpopular. None of these absolutely necessitated a divorce but there was a fourth that did. Catherine had not been able to provide Henry with a male child and was now presumed barren. There was a daughter, but competent statesmen were unanimous that a Queen on the throne of England was unthinkable. Anne and Henry were confident that between them they could produce a son; but if that son was to be Henry's heir, Anne would have to be Henry's wife.

The Pope was once again approached, this time by England only, and asked to declare the marriage with Catherine null, on the grounds that it contravened the Christian law which forbade marriage with a brother's widow. But England's insistence that the marriage had been null was now balanced by Spain's insistence that it hadn't. And at that moment Spain was well placed to influence the Pope's deliberations; Rome, where the Pope lived, had been very thoroughly sacked and occupied by Spanish troops. In addition one imagines a natural disinclination on the part of the Pope to have his powers turned on and off like a tap. At all events, after much ceremonious prevarication, while Henry waited with a rising temper, it became clear that so far as the Pope was concerned, the marriage with Catherine would stand.

To the ferment of a lover and the anxieties of a sovereign Henry now added a bad conscience; and a serious matter it was, for him and those about him.

The Bible, he found, was perfectly clear on such marriages as he had made with Catherine; they were forbidden. And the threatened penalty was exactly what had befallen him, the failure of male heirs. He was in a state of sin. He had been thrust into a state of sin by his father with the active help of the Pope. And the Pope now proposed to keep him in a state of sin. The man who would do that, it began to seem to Henry, had small claim to being the Vicar of God.

And indeed, on looking into the thing really closely, Henry found - what various voices had urged for centuries off and on - that the supposed Pope was no more than an ordinary Bishop, the Bishop of Rome. This made everything clear and everything possible. If the Pope was not a Pope at all but merely a bishop among bishops, then his special powers as Pope did not exist. In particular of course he had no power to dispense with

God's rulings as revealed in Leviticus 18, but equally important, he had no power to appoint other Bishops; and here an ancient quarrel stirred.

For if the Pope had not the power to appoint Bishops, then who did have, if not the King himself - King by the Grace of God? Henry's ancestors, all those other Henries, had been absolutely right; the Bishops of Rome, without a shadow of legality, had succeeded over the centuries in setting up a rival reign within the reign, a sort of long drawn usurpation. The very idea of it used to throw him into terrible rages. It should go on no longer.

He looked about for a good bishop to appoint to Canterbury, a bishop with no ambitions to modify God's ruling on deceased brother's wives, yet sufficiently spirited to grant a divorce to his sovereign without consulting the Bishop of Rome. The man was to hand in Thomas Cranmer; Catherine was divorced, Anne married, and the Established Church of England was off on its singular way.

This, very roughly indeed, is the political, or theological, or political-theological background to the play. But what of the social, or economic, or socio-economic, which we now think more important?

The economy was very progressive, the religion was very reactionary. We say therefore that the collision was inevitable, setting Henry aside as a colourful accident. With Henry presumably we set aside as accidents Catherine and Wolsey and Anne and More and Cranmer and Cromwell and the Lord Mayor of London and the man who cleaned his windows; setting indeed everyone advise as an accident, we say that the collision was inevitable. But that, on reflection, seems only to repeat that it happened. What is of interest is the way it happened, the way it was lived. For lived such collisions are. 'Religion' and 'economy' are abstractions which describe the way men live. Because men work we may speak of an economy, not the other way round. Because men worship we may speak of a religion, not the other way round. And when an economy collides with a religion it is living men who collide, nothing else (they collide with one another and within themselves).

Perhaps few people would disagree with that, put like that, and in theory. But in practice our theoreticians seem more and more to work the other way round, to derive the worker *from* his economy, the thinker *from* his culture, and we to derive even ourselves from our society and our location in it. When we ask ourselves 'What am I?' we may answer 'I am a Man' but are conscious that it's a silly answer because we don't know what kind of thing that might be; and feeling the answer silly we feel it's probably a silly question. We can't help asking it, however, for natural curiosity makes us ask it all the time of everyone else, and it would seem artificial to make ourselves the sole exception, would indeed envelop the mental image of our self in a unique silence and thus raise the question in a particularly disturbing way. So we answer of ourselves as we should of any other: 'This man here is a qualified surveyor, employed but with a view to partnership; this car he is driving has six cylinders and is almost new; he's doing all right; his opinions...' and so on, describing ourselves to ourselves in terms more appropriate to somebody seen through a window. We think of ourselves in the Third Person.

To put it another way, more briefly; we no longer have, as past societies have had, any picture of individual Man (Stoic Philosopher, Christian Religious, Rational Gentleman) by which to recognise ourselves and against which to measure ourselves; we are anything. But if anything, then nothing, and it is not everyone who can live with that, though it is our true present position. Hence our willingness to locate ourselves from something that is certainly larger than ourselves, the society that contains us.

But society can only have as much idea as we have what we are about, for it has only our brains to think with. And the individual who tries to plot his position by reference to our society finds no fixed points, but only the vaunted absence of them, 'freedom' and 'opportunity'; freedom for what, opportunity to do what, is nowhere indicated. The only positive he is given is 'get and spend' ('get and spend - if you can' from the Right, 'get and spend - you deserve it' from the Left) and he did not need society to tell him that. In other words we are thrown back by our society upon ourselves at our lowest, that is at our least satisfactory to ourselves. Which of course sends us flying back to society with all the force of rebound.

Socially, we fly from the idea of an individual to the professional describers, the classifiers, the men with the categories and a quick ear for the latest sub-division, who flourish among us like priests. Individually, we do what we can to describe and classify ourselves and so assure ourselves that from the outside at least we do have a definite outline. Both socially and individually it is with us as it is with our cities - an accelerating flight to the periphery, leaving a centre which is empty when the hours of business are over.

That is an ambitious style of thinking, and pride cometh before a fall, but it was with some such ideas in mind that I started on this play. Or else they developed as I wrote it. Or else I have developed them in defence of it now that it is written. It is not easy to know what a play is 'about' until it is finished, and by then what it is 'about' is incorporated in it irreversibly and is no more to be separated from it than the shape of a statue is to be separated from the marble. Writing a play is thinking, not thinking about thinking; more like a dream than a scheme - except that it lasts six months or more, and that one is responsible for it.

At any rate, Thomas More, as I wrote about him, became for me a man with an adamantine sense of his own self. He knew where he began and left off, what area of himself he could yield to the encroachments of his enemies, and what to the encroachments of those he loved. It was a substantial area in both cases for he had a proper sense of fear and was a busy lover. Since he was a clever man and a great lawyer he was able to retire from those areas in wonderfully good order, but at length he was asked to retreat from that final area where he located his self. And there this supple, humorous, unassuming and sophisticated person set like metal, was overtaken by an absolutely primitive rigour, and could no more be budged than a cliff.

This account of him developed as I wrote: what first attracted me was a person who could not be accused of any incapacity for life, who indeed seized life in great variety and almost greedy quantities, who nevertheless found something in himself without which life was valueless and when that was denied him was able to grasp his death. For there can be no doubt, given the circumstances, that he did it himself. If, on any day up to that of his execution, he had been willing to give public approval to Henry's marriage with Anne Boleyn, he could have gone on living. Of course the marriage was associated with other things - the attack on the abbeys, the whole Reformation policy - to which More was violently opposed, but I think he could have found his way round that; he showed every sign of doing so. Unfortunately his approval of the marriage was asked for in a form that required him to state that he believed what he didn't believe, and required him to state it on oath.

This brings me to something for which I feel the need to explain, perhaps apologise. More was a very orthodox Catholic and for him an oath was something perfectly specific; it was an invitation to God, an invitation God would not refuse, to act as a witness, and to judge; the consequence of perjury was damnation, for More another perfectly specific concept. So for More the issue was simple (though remembering the outcome it can hardly have been easy). But I am not a Catholic nor even in the meaningful sense of the word a Christian. So by what right do I appropriate a Christian Saint to my purposes? Or to put it the other way, why do I take as my hero a man who brings about his own death because he can't put his hand on an old black book and tell an ordinary lie?

For this reason: A man takes an oath only when he wants to commit himself quite exceptionally to the statement, when he wants to make an identity between the truth of it and his own virtue; he offers himself as a guarantee. And it works. There is a special kind of shrug for a perjurer; we feel that the man has no self to commit, no guarantee to offer. Of course it's much less effective now that for most of us the actual words of the oath are not much more than impressive mumbo-jumbo than it was when they made obvious sense; we would prefer most men to guarantee their statements with, say, cash rather than with themselves. We feel - we know - the self to be an equivocal commodity. There are fewer and fewer things which, as they say, we 'cannot bring ourselves' to do. We can find almost no limits for ourselves other than the physical, which being physical are not optional. Perhaps this is why we have fallen back so widely on physical torture as a means of bringing pressure to bear on one another. But though few of us have anything in ourselves like an immortal soul which we regard as absolutely inviolable, yet most of us still feel something which we should prefer, on the whole, not to violate. Most men feel when they swear an oath (the marriage vow for example) that they have invested something. And from this it's possible to guess what an oath must be to a man from whom it is not merely a time-honoured and understood ritual but also a definite contract. It may be that a clear sense of the self can *only* crystallise round something transcendental in which case, our prospects look poor, for we are rightly committed to the rational. I think the paramount gift our thinkers, artists, and for all I know, our men of science, should labour to get for us is a sense of selfhood without resort to magic. Albert Camus is a writer I admire in this connection.

Anyway, the above must serve as my explanation and apology for treating Thomas More, a Christian Saint, as a hero of selfhood.

Another thing that attracted me to this amazing man was his splendid social adjustment. So far from being one of society's sore teeth he was, like the hero of Camus' *La Chute,* almost indecently successful. He was respectably not nobly born, in the merchant class, the progressive class of the epoch, distinguished himself first as a scholar, then as a lawyer, was made an Ambassador, finally Lord Chancellor. A visitors' book at his house in Chelsea would have looked like a Sixteenth Century *Who's Who:* Holbein, Erasmus, Colet, everybody. He corresponded with the greatest minds in Europe as the representative and acknowledged champion of the New Learning in England. He was a friend of the King, who would send for More when his social appetites took a turn in that direction and once walked round the Chelsea garden with his arm round More's neck. ('If my head would win him a castle in France, it should not fail to fall,' said More.) He adored and was adored by his own large family. He parted with more than most men when he parted with his life, for he accepted and enjoyed his social context.

One sees that there is no necessary contradiction here; it is society after all which proffers an oath and with it the opportunity for perjury. But why did a man so utterly absorbed in his society, at one particular point disastrously part company from it? How indeed was it possible - unless there was some sudden aberration? But that explanation won't do, because he continued to the end to make familiar and confident use of society's weapons, tact, favour, and above all, the letter of the law.

For More again the answer to this question would be perfectly simple (though again not easy); the English Kingdom, his immediate society, was subservient to the larger society of the Church of Christ, founded by Christ, extending over Past and Future, ruled from Heaven. There are still some for whom that is perfectly simple, but for most it can only be a metaphor. I took it as a metaphor for that larger context which we all inhabit, the terrifying cosmos. Terrifying because no laws, no sanctions, no *mores* obtain there, it is either empty or occupied by God and Devil nakedly at war. The sensible man will seek to live his life without dealings with this larger environment, treating it as a fine spectacle on a clear night, or a subject for innocent curiosity. At the most he will allow himself an agreeable *frisson* when he contemplates his own relation to the cosmos, but he will not try to live in it; he will gratefully accept the shelter of his society. This was certainly More's intention.

If 'society' is the name we give to human behaviour when it is patterned and orderly, then the Law (extending from empirical traffic regulations, through the mutating laws of property, and on to the great tabus like incest and patricide) is the very pattern of society. More's trust in the law was his trust in his society; his desperate sheltering beneath the forms of the law was his determination to remain within the shelter of society. Cromwell's contemptuous shattering of the forms of law by an unconcealed act of perjury showed how fragile for any individual is that shelter. Legal or illegal had no further meaning, the social references had been removed. More was offered, to be sure, the chance of slipping back into the society which had thrust him out into the warring cosmos, but even in that solitude he found himself able to repeat, or continue, the decision he had made while he still enjoyed the common shelter.

I see that I have used a lot of metaphors. I know no other way to treat this subject. In the play I used for this theme a poetic image. As a figure for the superhuman context I took the largest, most alien, least formulated thing I know, the sea and water. The references to ships, rivers, currents, tides, navigation, and so on, are all used for this purpose. Society by contrast figures as dry land. I set out with no very well formed idea of the kind of play it was to be, except that it was not to be naturalistic. The possibility of using imagery, that is of using metaphors not decoratively but with an intention, was a side effect of that. It's a very far from new idea, of course. Whether it worked I rather doubt. Certainly no-one noticed. But I comfort myself with the thought that it's the nature of imagery to work, in performance at any rate, unconsciously. But if, as I think, a play is more like a poem than a straight narration, still less a demonstration or lecture, then imagery ought to be important. It's perhaps necessary to add that by a poem I mean something tough and precise, not something dreamy. As Brecht said, beauty and form of language are a primary alienation device. I was guaranteed some beauty and form by incorporating passages from Sir Thomas More himself. For the rest my concern was to match with these as best I could so that the theft should not be too obvious.

In two previous plays, *Flowering Cherry* and *The Tiger and the Horse,* I had tried, but with fatal timidity, to handle contemporaries in a style that should make them larger than life; in the first mainly by music and mechanical effects, in the second mainly by making the characters unnaturally articulate and unnaturally aware of what they 'stood for'. Inevitably these plays looked like what they most resembled, orthodox fourth wall drama with puzzling, uncomfortable, and, if you are uncharitable, pretentious overtones. So for this one I took a historical setting in the hope that the distance of years would give me Dutch courage, and enable me to treat my characters in a properly heroic, properly theatrical manner.

The style I eventually used was a bastardised version of the one most recently associated with Bertolt Brecht. This is not the place to discuss that style at any length, but it does seem to me that the style practised by Brecht differs from the style taught by Brecht, or taught to us by his disciples. Perhaps they are more Royalist than the King. Or perhaps there was something dæmonic in Brecht the artist which could not submit to Brecht the teacher. That would explain why in the *Chalk Circle,* which is to demonstrate that goodness is a terrible temptation, goodness triumphs very pleasantly. And why in *Mother Courage,* which is to demonstrate the unheroic nature of war, the climax is an act of heroism which Rider Haggard might have balked at. And why in *Galileo,* which is to demonstrate the social and objective value of scientific knowledge, Galileo, congratulated on saving his skin so as to argument that knowledge, is made to deny its value on the grounds that he defaulted at the moment when what the world needed was for one man to be true to himself. I am inclined to think that it is simply that Brecht was a very fine artist, and that life is complicated and ambivalent. At all events I agree with Eric Bentley that the proper effect of alienation is to enable the audience *reculer pour mieux sauter,* to deepen, not to terminate, their involvement in the play.

Simply to slap your audience in the face satisfies an austere and puritanical streak which runs in many of his disciples and sometimes, detrimentally I think, in Brecht himself. But it is a dangerous game to play. It has the effect of shock because it is unexpected. But it is unexpected only because it flies in the face of a thoroughly established convention. (A convention which goes far beyond naturalism; briefly, the convention that the actors are there as actors, not as themselves.) Each time it is done it is a little less unexpected, so that a bigger and bigger dosage will be needed to produce the same effect. If it were continued indefinitely it would finally not be unexpected at all. The theatrical convention would then have been entirely dissipated and we should have in the theatre a situation with one person who used to be an actor, desperately trying to engage the attention - by rude gestures, loud noises, indecent exposure, fireworks, anything - of other persons, who used to be the audience. As this point was approached some very lively evenings might be expected but the depth and subtlety of the notions which can be communicated by such methods may be doubted. When we use alienation methods just for kicks, we in the theatre are sawing through the branch on which we are sitting.

I tried then for a 'bold and beautiful verbal architecture', a story rather than a plot, and overtly theatrical means of switching from one locale to another. I also used the most notorious of the alienation devices, an actor who addresses the audience and comments on the action. But I had him address the audience in character, that is from within the play.

He is intended to draw the audience into the play, not thrust them off it. In this respect he largely fails, and for a reason I had not foreseen. He is called 'The Common Man' (just as there is a character called 'The King') and the word 'common' was intended primarily to indicate 'that which is common to us all'. But he was taken instead as a portrayal of that mythical beast The Man In The Street. This in itself was not so bad; after all he was intended to be something with which everyone would be able to identify. But once he was identified as common in that sense, my character was by one party accepted as a properly belittling account of that vulgar person, and by another party bitterly resented on his behalf (Myself I had meant him to be attractive, and his philosophy impregnable.) What both these parties had in common - if I may use the word - is that they thought of him as somebody else. Wherever he might have been, this Common Man, he was certainly not in the theatre. He is harder to find than a unicorn. But I must modify that. He was not in the Stalls, among his fashionable detractors and defenders. But in the laughter this character drew down from the Gallery, that laughter which is the most heartening sound our Theatre knows, I thought I heard once or twice a rueful note of recognition.

September 1960

A MAN FOR ALL SEASONS *was first presented in London at the Globe Theatre on 1st July 1960 by H.M. Tennent Ltd, with the following cast:*

THE COMMON MAN	Leo McKern
THOMAS MORE	Paul Scofield
RICHARD RICH	John Bown
THE DUKE	Alexander Gauge
ALICE MORE	Wynne Clark
MARGARET MORE	Pat Keen
THE CARDINAL	Willoughby Goddard
THOMAS CROMWELL	Andrew Keir
THE AMBASSADOR	Geoffrey Dunn
HIS ATTENDANT	Brian Harrison
WILLIAM ROPER	John Carson
THE KING	Richard Leech
A WOMAN	Beryl Andrews
THE ARCHBISHOP	William Roderick

The Play Directed by

NOËL WILLMAN

Scenery and costumes by

MOTLEY

PEOPLE IN THE PLAY

THE COMMON MAN: Late middle age. He wears from head to foot black tights which delineate his pot-bellied figure. His face is crafty, loosely benevolent, its best expression that of base humour.

SIR THOMAS MORE: Late forties. Pale, middle-sized, not robust. But the life of the mind in him is so abundant and debonair that it illuminates the body. His movements are open and swift but never wild, having a natural moderation. The face is intellectual and quickly delighted, the norm to which it returns serious and compassionate. Only in moments of high crisis does it become ascetic - though then freezingly.

RICHARD RICH: Early thirties. A good body unexercised. A studious unhappy face lit by the fire of banked down appetite. He is an academic, hounded by self-doubt to enter the world of affairs, and longing to be rescued from himself.

DUKE OF NORFOLK: Late forties. Heavy, active, a sportsman and soldier held together by rigid adherence to the minimal code of conventional duty. Attractively aware of his moral and intellectual insignificance, but also a great nobleman, untouchably convinced that his acts and ideas are important because they are his.

ALICE MORE: Late forties. Born into the merchant class, now a great lady, she is absurd at a distance, impressive close to. Overdressed, coarsely fashioned, she worships society; brave, hot-hearted, she worships her husband. In consequence, troubled by and defiant towards both.

MARGARET MORE: Middle twenties. A beautiful girl of ardent moral fineness; she both suffers and shelters behind a reserved stillness which it is her father's care to mitigate.

CARDINAL WOLSEY: Old. A big decayed body in scarlet. An almost megalomaniac ambition unhappily matched by an excelling intellect, he now inhabits a lonely den of self-indulgence and contempt.

THOMAS CROMWELL: Late thirties. Subtle and serious; the face expressing not inner tension but the tremendous out-going will of the Renaissance. A self-conceit that can cradle gross crimes in the name of effective action. In short an intellectual bully.

CHAPUYS: Sixties. A professional diplomat and lay ecclesiastic dressed in black. Much on his dignity as a man of the world he in fact trots happily along a mental footpath as narrow as a peasant's.

CHAPUYS' ATTENDANT: An apprentice diplomat of good family.

WILLIAM ROPER: Early thirties; a stiff body and an immobile face. Little imagination, moderate brain, but an all-consuming rectitude which is his cross, his solace, and his hobby.

THE KING: *Not* the Holbein Henry, but a much younger man, clean-shaven, bright-eyed, graceful and athletic. The Golden Hope of the New Learning throughout Europe. Only the levity with which he handles his absolute power foreshadows his future corruption.

A WOMAN: Middle fifties. Self-opinionated, self-righteous, selfish, indignant.

CRANMER: Late forties. Sharp-minded, sharp-faced. He treats the Church as a job of administration and theology as a set of devices, for he lacks personal religiosity.

THE SET is the same throughout but capable of varied lightings, as indicated. Its form is finally a matter for the designer, but to some extent is dictated by the action of the play. I have visualised two galleries of flattened Tudor arches, one above the other, able to be entered from off-stage. A flight of stairs leading from the upper gallery to the stage. A projection which can suggest an alcove or closet, with a tapestry curtain to be drawn across it. A table and some chairs, sufficiently heavy to be incongruous indoors or out.

THE COSTUMES are also a matter for the designer, but I have visualised no exact reproductions of the elaborate style of the period. I think plain colours should be used, thus scarlet for the Cardinal, grey for More, gold for the King, green for the Duke, blue for Margaret, black and pinstripe for the administrators Rich and Cromwell, and so on.

SIR THOMAS MORE

More is a man of an angel's wit and singular learning; I know not his fellow. For where is the man of that gentleness, lowliness, and affability? And as time requireth a man of marvellous mirth and pastimes; and sometimes of as sad gravity: a man for all seasons.

Robert Whittinton

A person of the greatest virtue this Kingdom ever produced.

Jonathan Swift

A MAN FOR ALL SEASONS

ACT ONE

When the curtain rises, the set is in darkness but for a single spot which descends vertically upon the COMMON MAN, *who stands in front of a big property basket.*

COMMON MAN   It is perverse! To start a play made up of Kings and Cardinals in speaking costumes and intellectuals with embroidered mouths, with me.

If a King, or a Cardinal had done the prologue he'd have had the right materials. And an intellectual would have shown enough majestic meanings, coloured propositions, and closely woven liturgical stuff to dress the House of Lords! But this!

Is this a costume? Does this say anything? It barely covers one man's nakedness! A bit of black material to reduce Old Adam to the Common Man.

Oh, if they'd let me come on naked, I could have shown you something of my own. Which would have told you without words — ! ... Something I've forgotten...Old Adam's muffled up.

(*Backing towards basket.*) Well, for a proposition of my own, I need a costume. (*Takes out and puts on the coat and hat of* STEWARD.)

Matthew! The Household Steward of Sir Thomas More! (*Lights come up swiftly on set. He takes from the basket five silver goblets, one larger than the others, and a jug with a lid, with which he furnishes the table. A burst of conversational merriment off; he pauses and indicates head of stairs.*) There's company to dinner. (*Finishes business at table.*)

All right! A Common Man! A Sixteenth-Century Butler! (*He drinks from the jug.*) All right — the Six — (*Breaks off, agreeably surprised by the quality of the liquor, regards the jug respectfully and drinks again.*) The Sixteenth Century is the Century of the Common Man. (*Puts down the jug.*) Like all the other centuries. (*Crossing right.*) And that's my proposition.

During the last part of the speech, voices off. Now, enter, at head of stairs, SIR THOMAS MORE.

STEWARD　That's Sir Thomas More.

MORE　The wine please, Matthew?

STEWARD　It's there, Sir Thomas.

MORE　(*looking into jug*) Is it good?

STEWARD　Bless you sir! *I* don't know.

MORE　(*mildly*) Bless you too, Matthew.

Enter RICH *at head of stairs.*

RICH　(*enthusiastically pursuing an argument*) But every man has his price!

STEWARD　(*contemptuous*) Master Richard Rich.

RICH　But yes! In money too.

MORE　(*gentle impatience*) No no no.

RICH　Or pleasure. Titles, women, bricks-and-mortar, there's always something.

MORE　Childish.

RICH　Well, in suffering, certainly.

MORE　(*interested*) Buy a man with suffering?

RICH　Impose suffering and offer him — escape.

MORE　Oh. For a moment I thought you were being profound.

(*Gives cup to* RICH.)

RICH　(*to* STEWARD) Good evening, Matthew.

STEWARD　(*snubbing*) 'Evening, sir.

RICH　No, not a bit profound; it then becomes a purely practical question of how to make him suffer sufficiently.

MORE　Mm… (*Takes him by the arm and walks with him.*) And … who recommended you to read Signor Machiavelli?

(RICH *breaks away laughing; a fraction too long.* MORE *smiles.*)

No, who? (*More laughter*)...Mm?

RICH   Master Cromwell.

MORE   Oh...(*Back to the wine jug and cups.*) He's a very able man.

RICH   And so he is!

MORE   Yes, I say he is. He's very able.

RICH   And he will do something for me, he says.

MORE   I didn't know you knew him.

RICH   Pardon me, Sir Thomas, but how much do you know about me?

MORE   Whatever you've let me know.

RICH   I've let you know everything!

MORE   Richard, you should go back to Cambridge; you're deteriorating.

RICH   Well, I'm not used! ... D'you know how much I have to show for seven month's work —

MORE   — Work?

RICH   Work! Waiting's work when you wait as I wait, hard!... For seven months, that's two hundred days, I have to show: the acquaintance of the Cardinal's outer doorman, the indifference of the Cardinal's inner doorman, and the Cardinal's chamberlain's hand in my chest!...Oh — also one half of a Good Morning delivered at fifty paces by the Duke of Norfolk. Doubtless he mistook me for someone.

MORE   He was very affable at dinner.

RICH   Oh, everyone's affable *here*... (MORE *is pleased.*) Also of course, the friendship of Sir Thomas More. Or should I say acquaintance?

MORE   Say friendship.

RICH   Well, there! 'A friend of Sir Thomas and still no office? There must be something wrong with him.'

MORE   I thought we said friendship... (*Considers; then*) The Dean of St Paul's offers you a post; with a house, a servant and fifty pounds a year.

RICH	What? What post?
MORE	At the new school.
RICH	(*bitterly disappointed*) A teacher!
MORE	A man should go where he won't be tempted. Look, Richard, see this. (*Hands a silver cup.*) Look ... Look ...
RICH	Beautiful.
MORE	Italian ... Do you want it?
RICH	Why — ?
MORE	No joke; keep it; or sell it.
RICH	Well I — Thank you of course — Thank you! Thank you! But — ?
MORE	You'll sell it, won't you?
RICH	Yes, I think so. Yes, I will.
MORE	And buy, what?
RICH	(*sudden ferocity*) Some decent clothes!
MORE	(*with sympathy*) Ah.
RICH	I want a gown like yours.
MORE	You'll get several gowns for that I should think. It was sent to me a little while ago by some woman. Now she's put a lawsuit into the Court of Requests. It's a bribe, Richard.
RICH	Oh ... (*Chagrined.*) So you give it away of course.
MORE	Yes!
RICH	To me?
MORE	Well, I'm not going to keep it, and you need it. Of course — if you feel it's contaminated ...
RICH	No no. I'll risk it. (*Both smile.*)
MORE	But, Richard, in office they offer you all sorts of things. I was once offered a whole village, with a mill, and a manor house, and heaven knows what else — a coat of arms I shouldn't be surprised. Why not be a teacher? You'd be a fine teacher. Perhaps, a great one.
RICH	And if I was who would know it?
MORE	You, your pupils, your friends, God. Not a bad public, that... Oh, and a *quiet* life.
RICH	(*laughing*) *You* say that!

MORE	Richard, I was commanded into office; it was inflicted on me…(RICH *regards him.*) Can't you believe that?
RICH	It's hard.
MORE	(*grimly*) Be a teacher.
	Enter at head of stairs NORFOLK.
STEWARD	(*to audience*) The Duke of Norfolk. A lord.
NORFOLK	I tell you he stooped from the clouds! (*Breaks off, irritable.*) Alice!
	Enter instantly at head of stairs ALICE.
ALICE	(*irritable*) Here!
STEWARD	(*to audience*) Lady Alice. My master's wife.
NORFOLK	I tell you he stooped —
ALICE	— He didn't —
NORFOLK	— Goddammit he did —
ALICE	— Couldn't —
NORFOLK	— He *does* —
ALICE	Not possible —
NORFOLK	— But *often* —
ALICE	— Never.
NORFOLK	Well, damn my soul! (*Takes wine.*) Thank you, Thomas.
MORE	(*to* MARGARET, *having appeared on gallery*) Come down, Meg.
STEWARD	(*to audience, soapy*) Lady Margaret, my master's daughter, lovely; really lovely.
ALICE	(*glances suspiciously at* STEWARD) Matthew, get about your business. (*Exit* STEWARD.) We'll settle this, my lord, we'll put it to Thomas. Thomas, no falcon could stoop from a cloud, could it?
MORE	I don't know, my dear, it sounds unlikely. I have seen falcons do some very splendid things.
ALICE	But how could he stoop from a cloud? He couldn't see where he was going.
NORFOLK	You see, Alice — you're ignorant of the subject; a real falcon don't *care* where he's going! Anyway, I'm talking

to Meg. (*A sportsman's story.*) 'Twas the very first cast of the day, Meg; the sun was behind us. And from side to side of the valley like the roof of a tent, was solid mist —

ALICE   Oh, mist.

NORFOLK   Well, mist is cloud isn't it?

ALICE   No.

RICH   The opinion of Aristotle is that mists are an exhalation of the earth whereas clouds —

NORFOLK   He stooped five hundred feet! Like *that!* Like an Act of God isn't he, Thomas?

MORE   He's tremendous.

NORFOLK   (*to* ALICE) Tremendous.

MARGARET   Did he kill the heron?

NORFOLK   Oh, the *heron* was *clever.* (*Very discreditable evidently.*) It was a royal stoop though. (*Sly.*) If you could ride, Alice, I'd show you.

ALICE   (*hotly*) I can ride, my lord!

MORE   No, no, you'll make yourself ill.

ALICE   And I'll bet — twenty-five — no thirty shillings I see no falcon stoop from no cloud!

NORFOLK   Done.

MORE   Alice — you can't ride with *them.*

ALICE   God's body, Thomas, remember who you are. Am I a City Wife?

MORE   No indeed, you've just lost thirty shillings I think; there *are* such birds. And the heron got home to his chicks, Meg, so everything was satisfactory.

MARGARET   (*smiling*) Yes.

MORE   What was that of Aristotle's, Richard?

RICHARD   Nothing, Sir Thomas — 'twas out of place.

NORFOLK   (*to* RICH) I've never found much use in Aristotle myself, not practically. Great philosopher of course. Wonderful mind.

RICH   Exactly, Your Grace!

NORFOLK   (*suspicious*) Eh?

MORE	Master Rich is newly converted to the doctrines of Machiavelli.
RICH	Oh *no*…!
NORFOLK	Oh, the Italian. Nasty book, from what I hear.
MARGARET	Very practical, Your Grace.
NORFOLK	You read it? Amazing girl, Thomas, but where are you going to find a husband for her?
MORE	(MORE *and* MEG *exchange a glance*) Where indeed?
RICH	The doctrines of Machiavelli have been largely mistaken I think; indeed properly apprehended he has no doctrine. Master Cromwell has the sense of it I think when he says —
NORFOLK	You know Cromwell?
RICH	… Slightly, Your Grace…
NORFOLK	The Cardinal's Secretary. (*Exclamations of shock from* MORE, MARGARET *and* ALICE.) It's a fact.
MORE	When, Howard?
NORFOLK	Two, three days.
	They move about uneasily.
ALICE	A *farrier's* son?
NORFOLK	Well, the Cardinal's a butcher's son, isn't he?
ALICE	It'll be up quick and down quick with Master Cromwell.
	NORFOLK *grunts.*
MORE	(*quietly*) Did you know this?
RICH	No!
MARGARET	Do you *like* Master Cromwell, Master Rich?
ALICE	He's the only man in London if he does!
RICH	I think I do, Lady Alice!
MORE	(*pleased*) Good… Well, you don't need *my* help now.
RICH	Sir Thomas, if only you knew how much, much rather I'd yours than his!
	Enter STEWARD *at head of stairs. Descends and gives letter to* MORE *who opens it and reads.*

MORE	Talk of the Cardinal's Secretary and the Cardinal appears. He wants me. Now.
ALICE	At this time of the night?
MORE	(*mildly*) The King's business.
ALICE	The Queen's business.
NORFOLK	More than likely, Alice, more than likely.
MORE	(*cuts in sharply*) What's the time?
STEWARD	Eleven o'clock, sir.
MORE	Is there a boat?
STEWARD	Waiting, sir.
MORE	(*To* ALICE *and* MARGARET) Go to bed. You'll excuse me, Your Grace? Richard? (*Kisses wife and daughter.*) Now you'll go to bed... (*The* MORE *family, as a matter of routine, put their hands together and*)
MORE ALICE MARGARET }	Dear Lord give us rest tonight, or if we must be wakeful, cheerful. Careful only for our soul's salvation. For Christ's sake. Amen.
MORE	And Bless our Lord the King.
ALICE MARGARET }	And Bless our Lord the King.
ALL	Amen
	And then immediately a brisk leave-taking, MORE *moving off below, the others mounting the stairs.*
MORE	Howard, are *you* at Richmond?
NORFOLK	No, down the river.
MORE	Then good night! (*Sees* RICH *disconsolate.*) Oh, Your Grace, here's a young man desperate for employment. Something in the clerical line.
NORFOLK	Well, if you recommend him.
MORE	No, I don't recommend him; but I point him out. (*Moving off.*) He's at the New Inn. You could take him there.
NORFOLK	(*to* RICH *mounting stairs*) All right, come on.
RICH	My Lord.
NORFOLK	We'll hawk at Hounslow, Alice.

ALICE	Wherever you like. (ALICE *and* MARGARET *follow* NORFOLK.)
RICH	(*at foot of stairs*) Sir Thomas!... (MORE *turns.*) Thank you.
MORE	Be a teacher. (*Moving off again.*) Oh − The ground's hard at Hounslow, Alice!
NORFOLK	Eh? (*Delighted roar.*) That's where the Cardinal crushed his bum!
MORE NORFOLK ALICE RICH }	Good night! Good night!

They process off along the gallery.

MORE	(*softly*) Margaret!
MARGARET	Yes?
MORE	Go to bed.

MARGARET *exits above*, MORE *exits below. After a moment* RICH *walks swiftly back down stage, picks up the goblet and is going off with it.*

STEWARD	Eh!
RICH	What − ! Oh... It's a gift, Matthew. Sir Thomas gave it to me. (STEWARD *takes it and regards it silently.*) He gave it to me.
STEWARD	(*returns it*) Very nice present, sir.
RICH	(*backing away with it*) Yes. Good night, Matthew.
STEWARD	Sir Thomas has taken quite a fancy to you, sir.
RICH	Er, here − (*Gives money and goes.*)
STEWARD	Thank you, sir ... (*To audience.*) That one'll come to nothing. (*Begins packing props into basket. Pauses with cup in hand.*) My master Thomas More would give anything to anyone. Some say that's good and some say that's bad, but I say he can't help it − and that's bad ... because some day someone's going to ask him for something that he wants to keep; and he'll be out of practice. (*Puts cloth with papers, ink, etc., on table.*) There must be something that he wants

to keep. That's only Common Sense.

Enter WOLSEY. *He sits at table and immediately commences writing, watched by* COMMON MAN *who then exits.*
Enter MORE.

WOLSEY (*writing*) It's half-past one. Where've you been?

(*Bell strikes one.*)

MORE One o'clock, Your Grace. I've been on the river.

WOLSEY *writes in silence, while* MORE *waits standing.*

WOLSEY (*still writing, pushes paper across table*) Since you seemed so violently opposed to the Latin dispatch, I thought you'd like to look it over.

MORE (*touched*) Thank you, Your Grace

WOLSEY Before it goes.

MORE (*smiles*) Your Grace is very kind. (*Takes and reads.*) Thank you.

WOLSEY Well, what d'you think of it? (*He is still writing.*)

MORE It seems very well phrased, Your Grace.

WOLSEY (*permits himself a chuckle*) The devil it does! (*Sits back.*)

And apart from the style, Sir Thomas?

MORE I think the Council should be told before that goes to Italy.

WOLSEY Would you tell the Council? Yes, I believe you would. You're a constant regret to me, Thomas. If you could just see facts flat on, without that moral squint; with just a little common sense, you could have been a statesman.

MORE (*little pause*) Oh, Your Grace flatters me.

WOLSEY Don't frivel... Thomas, are you going to help me?

MORE (*hesitates, looks away*) If Your Grace will be specific.

WOLSEY Ach, you're a plodder! Take you altogether, Thomas, your scholarship, your experience, what are you? (*A single trumpet calls, distant, frosty and clear.* WOLSEY *gets up and goes and looks from window.*) Come here. (MORE *joins him.*) The King.

MORE Yes.

WOLSEY	Where has he been? D'you know?
MORE	I, Your Grace?
WOLSEY	Oh, spare me your discretion. He's been to play in the muck again.
MORE	(*coldly*) Indeed.
WOLSEY	Indeed! Indeed! Are you going to oppose me?
	(*Trumpet again.* WOLSEY *visibly relaxes.*) He's gone in… (*Leaves window.*) All right, we'll plod. The King wants a son; what are you going to do about it?
MORE	(*dry murmur*) I'm very sure the King needs no advice from me on what to do about it.
WOLSEY	(*from behind grips his shoulder fiercely*) Thomas, we're alone. I give you my word. There's no one here.
MORE	I didn't suppose there was, Your Grace.
WOLSEY	Oh. (*Goes to table, sits, signs* MORE *to sit.* MORE *unsuspectingly obeys. Then, deliberately loud.*) Do you favour a change of dynasty, Sir Thomas? D'you think two Tudors is sufficient?
MORE	(*starting up in horrified alarm*) — For God's sake, Your Grace —!
WOLSEY	Then the King needs a son; I repeat what are you going to do about it?
MORE	(*steadily*) I pray for it daily.
WOLSEY	(*snatches up candle and holds to* MORE'S *face. Softly*) God's death, he means it… That thing out there's at least fertile, Thomas.
MORE	But she's not his wife.
WOLSEY	No, Catherine's his wife and she's as barren as brick. Are you going to pray for a miracle?
MORE	There *are* precedents.
WOLSEY	Yes. All right. Good. Pray. Pray by all means. But in addition to Prayer there is Effort. My effort's to secure a divorce. Have I your support or have I not?
MORE	(*sits*) A dispensation was given so that the King might marry Queen Catherine, for state reasons. Now we are to

ask the Pope to — dispense with his dispensation, also for
state reasons?

WOLSEY — I don't *like* plodding, Thomas, don't make me plod
longer than I have to — Well?

MORE Then, clearly all we have to do is approach His Holiness
and ask him.

The pace becomes rapid.

WOLSEY — I think we might influence His Holiness' answer —

MORE — Like this? — (*The dispatch.*)

WOLSEY — Like that and in other ways —

MORE — I've already expressed my opinion on this —

WOLSEY — Then, good night! Oh, your conscience is your own
affair; but you're a statesman! Do you *remember* the
Yorkist Wars?

MORE Very clearly.

WOLSEY Let him die without an heir and we'll have them
back again. Let him die without an heir and this
'peace' you think so much of will go out like that!
(*Extinguishes candle.*) Very well, then England
needs an heir; certain measures, perhaps regrettable,
perhaps not — (*pompous*) there is much in the
Church that *needs* reformation, Thomas — (MORE
smiles.) All right, regrettable! But necessary, to
get us an heir! Now explain how you as Councillor
of England can obstruct those measures for the
sake of your own, private, conscience.

MORE Well … I believe, when statesmen forsake their own
private conscience for the sake of their public duties
… they lead their country by a short route to chaos.
(*During this speech he relights the candle with
another.*) And we shall have my prayers to fall
back on.

WOLSEY You'd like that, wouldn't you? To govern the country
by prayers?

MORE Yes, I should.

WOLSEY I'd like to be there when you try. Who *will* deal

with all this — paper, after me? You? Fisher? Suffolk?

MORE   Fisher for me.

WOLSEY Aye, but for the King. What about my Secretary, Master Cromwell?

MORE   Cromwell!

WOLSEY You'd rather do it yourself?

MORE   Me rather than Cromwell.

WOLSEY Then come down to earth … And until then, allow for an enemy, here!

MORE   As Your Grace pleases.

WOLSEY As God wills!

MORE   Perhaps, Your Grace. (*Mounting stairs.*)

WOLSEY More! You should have been a cleric!

MORE   (*amused, looking down from gallery*) Like yourself, Your Grace?

Exit MORE. WOLSEY *is left staring, then exits through the lower arches with candle, taking most of the light from the stage as he does so. But the whole rear of the stage now patterns with webbed reflections thrown from brightly moonlit water, so that the structure is thrown into black relief, while a strip of light descends along the front of the stage, which is to be the acting area for the next scene.*

An oar and a bundle of clothing are lowered into this area from above. Enter COMMON MAN; *he unties the bundle and dons the coat and hat of* BOATMAN.

MORE   (*off*) Boat! (*Approaching.*) Boat!

BOATMAN (*donning coat and hat*) Here, sir!

MORE   (*off*) A boatman please!

BOATMAN Boat here, sir! (*He seizes the oar.*)

        Enter MORE.

MORE   (*peering*) Boatman?

BOATMAN	Yes, sir. (*To audience, indicating oar.*) A boatman.
MORE	Take me home.
BOATMAN	(*pleasantly*) I was just going home myself, sir.
MORE	Then find me another boat.
BOATMAN	Bless you, sir — that's all right! (*Comfortably.*) I expect you'll make it worth my while, sir.

CROMWELL *steps from behind arch, left.*

CROMWELL	Boatman, have you a licence?
BOATMAN	Eh? Bless you, sir, yes; I've got a licence.
CROMWELL	Then you know that the fares are fixed — (*Turns to* MORE. *Exaggerated pleasure.*) Why, it's Sir Thomas!
MORE	Good morning, Master Cromwell. You work very late.
CROMWELL	I'm on my way to the Cardinal. (*He expects an answer.*)
MORE	Ah.
CROMWELL	You have just left him I think.
MORE	Yes, I have.
CROMWELL	You left him … in his laughing mood, I hope?
MORE	On the whole I would say, not. No, not laughing.
CROMWELL	Oh, I'm sorry. (*Backing to exit.*) I am one of your *multitudinous* admirers, Sir Thomas. A penny ha'penny to Chelsea, Boatman.

Exit CROMWELL.

BOATMAN	The coming man they say, sir.
MORE	Do they? Well, where's your boat?
BOATMAN	Just along the wharf, sir.

They are going, when enter CHAPUYS *and* ATTENDANT *from archway, Right.*

CHAPUYS	Sir Thomas More!
MORE	Signor Chapuys? You're up very late, Your Excellency.
CHAPUYS	(*significantly*) So is the Cardinal, Sir Thomas.
MORE	(*closing up*) He sleeps very little.
CHAPUYS	You have just left him, I think.
MORE	You are correctly informed. As always.

CHAPUYS I will not ask you the subject of your conversation.

... (*He waits.*)

MORE No, of course not.

CHAPUYS Sir Thomas, I will be plain with you ... plain, that is, so far as the diplomatic decencies permit. (*Loudly.*) My master Charles, the King of Spain! (*Pulls* MORE *aside, discreet.*) My master Charles, the King of Spain, feels himself concerned in anything concerning his blood relation! He would feel himself insulted by any insult offered to his father's sister! I refer of course to Queen Catherine. (*Regards* MORE, *keenly.*) The King of Spain would feel himself insulted by any insult offered to Queen Catherine.

MORE His feeling would be natural.

CHAPUYS (*consciously sly*) Sir Thomas, may I ask if you and the Cardinal parted, how shall I say, amicably?

MORE Amicably... Yes.

CHAPUYS (*a shade indignant*) In agreement?

MORE Amicably.

CHAPUYS (*warmly*) Say no more, Sir Thomas; I understand.

MORE (*a shade worried*) I hope you do, Your Excellency.

CHAPUYS You are a good man.

MORE I don't see how you deduce that from what I've told you.

CHAPUYS (*holds up hand*) A nod is as good as a wink to a blind horse. I understand. You are a good man. (*Turns to exit.*) Dominus vobiscum.

Exit CHAPUYS. MORE *looks after him. Then:*

MORE (*abstracted*)... spiritu tuo ...

BOATMAN (*mournful; he is squatting on the ground*) People seem to think boats stay afloat on their own, sir, but they don't; they cost money. (MORE *is abstractedly gazing over the audience.*) Take anchor rope, sir, you may not believe me for a little skiff like mine, but it's a penny a fathom. (MORE *is still abstracted.*) And with a young wife, sir, as you know ...

MORE (*abstracted*) I'll pay what I always pay you... The river

	looks very black tonight. They say it's silting up, is that so?
BOATMAN	(*joining him*) Not in the middle, sir. There's a channel there getting deeper all the time.
MORE	How is your wife?
BOATMAN	She's losing her shape, sir, losing it fast.
MORE	Well, so are we all.
BOATMAN	Oh yes, sir; it's common.
MORE	(*going*) Well, take me home.
	Exit MORE.
BOATMAN	That I will, sir! (*Crossing to basket and pulling it out.*) From Richmond to Chelsea, downstream, a penny half-penny … coat, hat (*goes for table-cloth*) from Chelsea to Richmond, upstream, a penny halfpenny. Whoever makes the regulations doesn't row a boat. Cloth … (*Puts cloth in basket, takes out slippers.*) Home again.
	Lighting changes to MORE'S *house interior.*
	Enter MORE *on stairs. Sits wearily. Takes off hat, half takes off coat, but is too tired. It chimes three.* STEWARD *kneels to put on his slippers for him.*
MORE	Ah, Matthew… Thank you. Is Lady Alice in bed?
STEWARD	Yes, sir.
MORE	Lady Margaret?
STEWARD	No, sir. Master Roper's here.
MORE	(*surprised*) At this hour? … Who let him in?
STEWARD	He's a hard man to keep out, sir.
MORE	Where are they?
	Enter MARGARET *and* ROPER,
MARGARET	Here, Father.
MORE	(*regarding them, resignedly*) Good morning, William. It's a little early for breakfast.
ROPER	(*solidly*) I haven't come for breakfast, sir.
	MORE *looks at him and sighs.*
MARGARET	Will wants to marry me, Father.
MORE	Well, he can't marry you.
ROPER	Sir Thomas, I'm to be called to the Bar.

MORE   (*warmly*) Oh, congratulations, Roper!

ROPER   My family may not be at the palace, sir, but in the City —

MORE   The Ropers were advocates when the Mores were selling pewter; there's nothing wrong with your family. There's nothing wrong with your fortune — there's nothing wrong with you — (*sourly*) except you need a clock —

ROPER   I can buy a clock, sir.

MORE   Roper, the answer's 'no'. (*Firmly.*) And will be 'no' so long as you're a heretic.

ROPER   (*firing*) That's a word I don't like, Sir Thomas!

MORE   It's not a likeable word. (*Coming to life.*) It's not a likeable thing!

> MARGARET *is alarmed, and from behind* MORE *tries to silence* ROPER.

ROPER   The Church is heretical! Doctor Luther's proved that to my satisfaction!

MORE   Luther's an excommunicate.

ROPER   From a heretic Church! Church? It's a shop — Forgiveness by the florin! Joblots now in Germany! … Mmm, and divorces.

MORE   (*expressionless*) Divorces?

ROPER   Oh, half England's buzzing with that.

MORE   'Half England.' The Inns of Court may be buzzing, England doesn't buzz so easily.

ROPER   It will. And is that a Church? Is that a Cardinal? Is that a Pope? Or Antichrist! (MORE *looks up angrily.* MARGARET *signals frantically.*) Look, what I know I'll say!

MARGARET   You've no sense of the *place!*

MORE   (*rueful*) He's no sense of the time.

ROPER   I — (*But* MORE *gently holds up his hand and he stops.*)

MORE   Listen, Roper. Two years ago you were a passionate Churchman; now you're a passionate — Lutheran. We must just pray, that when your head's finished turning your face is to the front again.

ROPER	Don't lengthen your prayers with *me,* sir!
MORE	Oh, one more or less … Is your horse here?
ROPER	No, I walked.
MORE	Well, take a horse from the stables and get back home. (ROPER *hesitates.*) Go along.
ROPER	May I come again? (MORE *indicates* MARGARET.)
MARGARET	Yes. Soon.
ROPER	Good night, sir.
	Exit ROPER
MARGARET	Is that final, Father?
MORE	As long as he's a heretic, Meg, that's absolute. (*Warmly*). Nice boy… Terribly strong principles though. I told you to go to bed.
MARGARET	Yes, why?
MORE	(*lightly*) Because I intended you to *go* to bed. You're very pensive?
MARGARET	You're very gay. Did he talk about the divorce?
MORE	Mm? You know I think we've been on the wrong track with Will — It's no good arguing with a Roper —
MARGARET	Father, did he?
MORE	*Old* Roper was just the same. Now let him think he's going *with* the current and he'll turn round and start swimming in the opposite direction. What we want is a really substantial attack on the Church.
MARGARET	We're going to get it, aren't we?
MORE	Margaret, I'll not have you talk treason … And I'll not have you repeat lawyer's gossip. I'm a lawyer myself and I know what it's worth.
ALICE	(*off. Indignant and excited*) Thomas — !
MORE	Now look what you've done.
	Enter ALICE *at head of stairs in nightgown.*
ALICE	Young Roper! I've just seen young Roper! On *my* horse.
MORE	He'll bring it back, dear. He's been to see Margaret.
ALICE	Oh — why you don't beat that girl!

MORE   No no, she's full of education — and it's a delicate commodity.

ALICE   Mm! And more's the pity!

MORE   Yes, but it's there now and think what it cost. (*He sneezes.*)

ALICE   (*pouncing*) Ah! Margaret — hot water.

Exit MARGARET.

MORE   I'm sorry you were awakened, chick.

ALICE   I wasn't sleeping very deeply. Thomas — what did Wolsey want?

MORE   (*innocent*) Young Roper asked for Margaret.

ALICE   What! Impudence!

MORE   Yes, wasn't it?

ALICE   Old fox! What did he want, Thomas?

MORE   He wanted me to read a dispatch.

ALICE   Was that all?

MORE   A Latin dispatch.

ALICE   Oh! Won't you talk about it?

MORE   (*gently*) No.

Enter MARGARET *with cup which she takes to* MORE.

ALICE   Norfolk was speaking for you as Chancellor before he left.

MORE   He's a dangerous friend then. Wolsey's Chancellor, God help him. We don't want another. (MARGARET *takes cup to him; he sniffs it.*) I don't want this.

ALICE   Drink it. Great men get colds in the head just the same as commoners.

MORE   That's dangerous, levelling talk, Alice. Beware of the Tower. (*Rises.*) I will, I'll drink it in bed.

All move to stairs and ascend, talking.

MARGARET   Would you want to be Chancellor?

MORE   No.

MARGARET   That's what I said. But Norfolk said if Wolsey fell —

MORE   (*no longer flippant*) If Wolsey fell, the splash would swamp a few small boats like ours. There will be no new Chancellors while Wolsey lives.

Exit above.

The light is dimmed there and a bright spot descends below. Into this bright circle from the wings is thrown the great red robe and the Cardinal's hat. The COMMON MAN *enters from the opposite wing and roughly piles them into his basket. He then takes from his pocket a pair of spectacles and from the basket a book. He reads:*

COMMON MAN
(*reading*) 'Whether we follow tradition in ascribing Wolsey's death to a broken heart, or accept Professor Larcomb's less feeling diagnosis of pulmonary pneumonia, its effective cause was the King's displeasure. He died at Leicester on 29 November 1530 while on his way to the Tower under charge of High Treason.
'England's next Lord Chancellor was Sir Thomas More, a scholar and, by popular repute, a saint. His scholarship is supported by his writings; saintliness is a quality less easy to establish. But from his wilful indifference to realities which were obvious to quite ordinary contemporaries, it seems all too probable that he had it.'

Exit COMMON MAN. *As he goes, lights come up and a screen is lowered depicting Hampton Court.* CROMWELL *is sitting halfway up the stairs.*

Enter RICH, *crossing.*

CROMWELL
Rich! (RICH *stops, sees him, and smiles willingly.*)

What brings you to Hampton?

RICH
I came with the Duke last night, Master Cromwell. They're hunting again.

CROMWELL
It's a kingly pastime, Master Rich. (*Both smile.*) I'm glad you found employment. You're the Duke's Secretary are you not?

RICH
(*flustered*) My work *is* mostly secretarial.

CROMWELL
(*as one making an effort of memory*) Or is it his librarian you are?

RICH
I do look after His Grace's library, yes.

CROMWELL   Oh. Well, that's something. And I don't suppose you're
bothered much by His Grace — in the library? (RICH *smiles
uncertainly.*) It's odd how differently men's fortunes flow.
My late master died in disgrace, and here I am in the King's
own service. There you are in a *comparative* backwater —
yet the new Lord Chancellor's an old friend of yours.

(He looks at him directly.)

RICH   (*uncertainly*) He isn't really my *friend* ...

CROMWELL   Oh, I thought he was. (*Gets up, prepares to go.*)

RICH   — In a sense he is.

CROMWELL   (*reproachful*) Well, I always understood he set you up in
life.

RICH   Master Cromwell — what *is* it that you do for the King?

Enter CHAPUYS.

CHAPUYS   (*roguish*) Yes, *I* should like to know that, Master Cromwell.

CROMWELL   Ah, Signor Chapuys. You've met His Excellency, Rich?
(*Indicates* CHAPUYS.) The Spanish Ambassador. (*Indicates*
RICH.) The Duke of Norfolk's librarian.

CHAPUYS   But how should we introduce *you,* Master Cromwell, if we
had the happiness?

CROMWELL   Oh sly! Do you notice how sly he is, Rich?
(*Walks away.*) Well, I suppose you would call me
(*suddenly turns*) 'The King's Ear'... (*Deprecating
shrug.*) It's a useful organ, the ear. But in fact it's
even simpler than that. When the King wants
something done, I do it.

CHAPUYS   Ah. (*Mock interest.*) But then why these Justices,
Chancellors, Admirals?

CROMWELL   Oh, *they* are the constitution. Our ancient, English
constitution. I merely do things.

CHAPUYS   For example, Master Cromwell...

CROMWELL   (*admiring*) Oho — beware these professional diplomats.
Well now, for example; next week at Deptford we are
launching the *Great Harry* — one thousand tons, four
masts, sixty-six guns, an overall length of one hundred and

seventy-five feet, it's expected to be very effective —
all this you probably know. However you may not
know that the King himself will guide her down the
river; yes, the King himself will be her pilot. He will
have assistance of course but he himself will be her
pilot. He will have a pilot's whistle upon which he
will blow, and he will wear in every respect a
common pilot's uniform. Except for the material,
which will be cloth of gold. These innocent fancies
require more preparation than you might suppose
and someone has to do it. (*He spreads his hands.*)
Meanwhile, I do prepare myself for, higher things.
I stock my mind.

CHAPUYS   Alas, Master Cromwell, don't we all? This ship for
instance — it has fifty-six guns by the way, not
sixty-six and only forty of them heavy — After the
launching I understand, the King will take his
barge to Chelsea. (CROMWELL'S *face darkens during
this speech.*)

CROMWELL   (*sharply*) Yes —

CHAPUYS   — To —

CROMWELL}
CHAPUYS}   (*together*) Sir Thomas More's.

CHAPUYS   (*sweetly*) Will you be there?

CROMWELL   Oh, no — they'll talk about the divorce. (*It is* CHAPUYS' *turn
to be shocked:* RICH *draws away uneasily.*) The King will
ask him for an answer.

CHAPUYS   (*ruffled*) He has given his answer!

CROMWELL   The King will ask him for another.

CHAPUYS   Sir Thomas is a good son of the Church!

CROMWELL   Sir Thomas is a man.

Enter STEWARD. *Both* CROMWELL *and* CHAPUYS *look towards
him sharply, then back at one another.*

CHAPUYS   (*innocently*) Isn't that his Steward now?

CROMWELL   I believe it is. Well, good day, Your Excellency.

CHAPUYS   (*eager*) Good day, Master Cromwell. (*He expects
him to go.*)

CROMWELL (*standing firm*) Good day. (*And* CHAPUYS *has to go.*)

CROMWELL *walks side stage, with furtive and urgent beckonings to* STEWARD *to follow.* RICH *follows but hangs off. Meanwhile* CHAPUYS *and his* ATTENDANT *have gone behind screen, beneath which their legs protrude clearly.*

STEWARD (*conspiratorial*) Sir, Sir Thomas doesn't talk about it. (*He waits but* CROMWELL *remains stony.*) He doesn't talk about it, to his wife, sir. (*He waits again.*)

CROMWELL This is worth nothing.

STEWARD (*significant*) But he doesn't talk about it to Lady Margaret — that's his daughter, sir.

CROMWELL So?

STEWARD So he's worried, sir... (CROMWELL *is interested.*) Frightened ... (CROMWELL *takes out a coin but pauses suspiciously.*) Sir, he goes *white* when it's mentioned!

CROMWELL (*hands coin*) All right.

STEWARD (*looks at coin; reproachful*) Oh, sir — !

CROMWELL (*waves him away*) Are you coming in my direction, Rich?

RICH (*still hanging off*) No no.

CROMWELL I think you should, you know.

RICH *I* can't tell you anything!

Exit RICH *and* CROMWELL *left and right.* CHAPUYS *and* ATTENDANT *come from behind screen.*

CHAPUYS (*beckons* STEWARD) Well?

STEWARD Sir Thomas rises at six, sir, and prays for an hour and a half.

CHAPUYS Yes?

STEWARD During Lent, sir, he lived entirely on bread and water.

CHAPUYS Yes?

STEWARD He goes to confession twice a week, sir. Parish priest. Dominican.

CHAPUYS Ah. He is a true son of the Church.

STEWARD	(*soapy*) That he is, sir.
CHAPUYS	What did Master Cromwell want?
STEWARD	Same as you, sir.
CHAPUYS	No man can serve two masters, Steward.
STEWARD	No, indeed, sir; I serve *one*. (*He pulls to the front an enormous cross until then hanging at his back on a length of string — a caricature of the ebony cross worn by* CHAPUYS.)
CHAPUYS	Good, simple man. Here. (*Gives coin. Going.*) Peace be with you.
STEWARD	And with you, sir.
CHAPUYS	Our Lord watch you.
STEWARD	You too, sir. (*Exit* CHAPUYS.) That's a very religious man.
	Enter RICH.
RICH	What does Signor Chapuys want, Matthew?
STEWARD	I've no idea, sir.
RICH	(*gives coin*) What did you tell him?
STEWARD	I told him that Sir Thomas says his prayers and goes to confession.
RICH	Why that?
STEWARD	That's what he wanted to know, sir. I mean I could have told him any number of things about Sir Thomas — that he has rheumatism, prefers red wine to white, is easily sea-sick, fond of kippers, afraid of drowning. But that's what he wanted to know, sir.
RICH	What did he say?
STEWARD	He said that Sir Thomas is a good churchman, sir.
RICH	(*going*) Well, that's true, isn't it?
STEWARD	I'm just telling you what he said, sir. Master Cromwell went that way, sir.
RICH	(*furious*) Did I ask you which way Master Cromwell went?
	Exit RICH *opposite.*
STEWARD	(*to audience, thoughtfully*) The great thing's not to get out of your depth … What I can tell them's common

knowledge! But now they've given money for it and everyone wants value for his money. They'll make a secret of it now to prove they've not been bilked....They'll make it a secret by making it dangerous....Mm....Oh, when I can't touch the bottom I'll go deaf blind and dumb. (*Holds out coins.*) And that's more than I *earn* in a fortnight!

On this, a fanfare of trumpets; plainsong; the rear of the stage becomes a source of glittering blue light; Hampton Court is hoisted out of sight, and other screens are lowered one after the other, each masking the rest, bearing respectively sunflowers, hollyhocks, roses, magnolias. When the fanfare ceases the plainsong goes on quietly, and the screens throw long shadows like the shadows of trees, and NORFOLK, ALICE, MARGARET, *erupt on to the stage.*

ALICE (*distressed*) No sign of him, my lord!

NORFOLK God's body, Alice, he must be found!

ALICE (*to* MEG) He *must* be in the house!

MARGARET He's *not* in the house, Mother!

ALICE Then he must be here in the garden!

They 'search' among the screens.

NORFOLK He takes things too far, Alice.

ALICE Do I not know it?

NORFOLK It will end badly for him!

ALICE I know that too!

They 'notice' the STEWARD.

MARGARET ⎱
ALICE ⎬ (*together*) ⎰ Matthew! Where's my father?
NORFOLK ⎰ Where is Sir Thomas?
Where's your master?

Fanfare, shorter but nearer.

NORFOLK (*despairing*) Oh my God.

ALICE Oh Jesus!

STEWARD My lady — the King?

NORFOLK Yes, fool! (*Threatening.*) And if the King arrives and the Chancellor's not here —

STEWARD Sir, my lady, it's not *my* fault!

NORFOLK (*quietly displeased*) Lady Alice, Thomas'll get no

good of it. This is not how Wolsey made himself great.

ALICE   (*stiffly*) Thomas has his own way of doing things, my lord!

NORFOLK   (*testy*) Yes yes, Thomas is unique; but where *is* Thomas?

STEWARD *swings onstage small gothic door. Plainsong. All run to the door.* NORFOLK *opens it.*

ALICE   Thomas!

STEWARD   Sir!

MARGARET   Father!

NORFOLK   (*indignant*) My Lord Chancellor!

Enter MORE *through the doorway. He blinks in the light. He is wearing a cassock. Shuts door behind him.*

What sort of fooling is this? Does the King visit you every day.

MORE   No, but I go to Vespers most days.

NORFOLK   He's here!

MORE   But isn't this visit *meant* to be a surprise?

NORFOLK   (*grimly*) For you, yes, not for him.

MARGARET   Father… (*Indicates cassock.*)

NORFOLK   Yes — d'you propose to meet the King disguised as a parish clerk? (*They fall upon him and drag the cassock over his head.*) A parish clerk, my lord Chancellor! You dishonour the King and his office!

MORE   (*appearing momentarily in the folds of the cassock*) The service of God is not a dishonour to any office. (*The cassock is pulled off.*) Believe me, my friend, I do not belittle the honour His Majesty is doing me. (*Briskly.*) Well! That's a lovely dress, Alice; so's that, Margaret. (*Looks at* NORFOLK.) I'm a dowdy bird, aren't I? (*Looks at* ALICE.) Calm yourself, Alice, we're all ready now.

He turns about and we see that his gown is caught up behind him revealing his spindly legs in long hose laced up at the thighs.

ALICE   Thomas!

MARGARET *laughs.*

MORE	What's the matter? (*Turns round again and his women folk pursue him to pull down the gown while* NORFOLK *throws his hands in the air. Expostulation, explanation, exclamation, overlapping in a babble.*)
NORFOLK	— By God you can be hare-brained — !
MARGARET	— Be still — !
ALICE	— Oh, Thomas! Thomas! —
NORFOLK	— What whim possessed you —
MORE	— 'Twas not a whim — !
ALICE	— Your second best stockings — !
MARGARET	— Father, be still — !
NORFOLK	— Oh, enough's enough — !
MORE	— Haven't you done — !

HENRY, *in a cloth of gold, runs out of the sunlight half-way down the steps, and blows a blast on his pilot's whistle. All kneel. In the silence he descends slowly to their level, blowing softly …*

MORE	Your Majesty does my house more honour than I fear my household can bear.
HENRY	No ceremony, Thomas! No ceremony! (*They rise.*) A passing fancy — I happened to be on the river. (*Holds out shoe, proudly.*) Look, mud.
MORE	We do it in better style, Your Grace, when we come by the road.
HENRY	Oh, the road! There's the road for me, Thomas, the river, *my* river … By heaven what an evening! I fear we come upon you unexpectedly, Lady Alice.
ALICE	(*shocked*) Oh no, Your Grace — (*remembering*) that is yes, but we are ready for you — ready to entertain Your Grace that is.
MORE	This is my daughter Margaret, sir. She has not had the honour to meet Your Grace. (*She curtseys low.*)
HENRY	(*looks her over, then*) Why, Margaret, they told me you were a scholar.

MARGARET *is confused.*

MORE	Answer, Margaret.

MARGARET   Among women I pass for one Your Grace.

             NORFOLK *and* ALICE *exchange approving glances.*

HENRY   Antiquone modo Latine loqueris, an Oxoniensi?

             [Is your Latin the old Latin, or Oxford Latin?]

MARGARET   Quem me docuit pater, Domine.

             [My father's Latin, Sire.]

HENRY   Bene. Optimus est. Graecamne linguam quoque te docuit?

             [Good. That is the best. And has he taught you Greek too?]

MARGARET   Graecam me docuit non pater meus sed mei patris amicus,
             Johannes Coletus, Sancti Pauli Decanus. In litteris Graecis
             tamen, non minus quam Latinis, ars magistri minuitur
             discipuli stultitia.

             [Not my father, Sire, but my father's friend, John Colet,
             Dean of St Paul's. But it is with the Greek as it is with the
             Latin; the skill of the master is lost in the pupil's lack of it.]

             Her Latin is better than his; he is not altogether pleased.

HENRY   Ho! (*He walks away from her, talking; she begins to rise
             from her curtsey,* MORE *gently presses her down again
             before the King turns.*) Take care, Thomas: 'There is no
             end to the making of books and too much reading is a
             weariness of the flesh.' (*Back to* MARGARET.) Can you dance,
             too?

MARGARET   Not well, Your Grace.

HENRY   Well, *I* dance superlatively! (*Plants his leg before her face.*)
             That's a dancer's *leg,* Margaret! (*She has the wit to look
             straight up and smile at him. All good humour he pulls
             her to her feet; sees* NORFOLK *grinning the grin of a
             comrade.*) Hey, Norfolk? (*Indicates* NORFOLK'S *leg with
             much distaste.*) Now *that's* a wrestler's leg. But I can
             throw him. (*Seizes* NORFOLK.) Shall I show them, Howard?
             (NORFOLK *is alarmed for his dignity. To* MARGARET.) Shall I?

MARGARET   (*looking at* NORFOLK, *gently*) No, Your Grace.

HENRY   (*releases* NORFOLK, *seriously*) You are gentle. (*To* MORE,
             approving.) That's good. (*To* MARGARET.) You shall read to
             me.   (MARGARET *is about to demur.*)   No no, you shall

read to me. Lady Alice, the river's given me an appetite.

ALICE   If Your Grace would share a very simple supper.

HENRY   It would please me to. (*Preparing to lead off, sees* MARGARET *again.*) I'm something of a scholar too; did you know?

MARGARET   All the world knows Your Grace's Book, asserting the seven sacraments of the Church.

HENRY   Ah yes. Between ourselves, your father had a hand in that; eh, Thomas?

MORE   Here and there, Your Grace. In a minor capacity.

HENRY   (*looking at him*) He seeks to shame me with his modesty ... (*Turns to* ALICE.) On second thoughts we'll follow, Lady Alice, Thomas and I will follow. (*He waves them off. They bow, withdraw, prepare for second bow.*) Wait! (*Raises whistle to lips; then*) Margaret, are you fond of music?

MARGARET   Yes, Your Grace.

HENRY   (*beckons her to him; holds out whistle*) Blow. (*She is uncertain.*) Blow. (*She does.*) Louder! (*She does and at once music without, stately and oversweet. Expressions of pleasure all round.*) I brought them with me, Lady Alice; take them in! (*Exit all but* MORE *and* HENRY. *The music continues receding.*) Listen to this, Thomas. (*He walks about, the auditor, beating time.*) Do you know it?

MORE   No, Your Grace, I —

HENRY   Sh! (MORE *is silent;* HENRY *goes on with his listening.*) ... I launched a ship today, Thomas.

MORE   Yes, Your Grace, I —

HENRY   *Listen,* man, *listen* ... (*A silence*)... The *Great Harry* ... I steered her, Thomas, under sail.

MORE   You have many accomplishments, Your Grace.

HENRY   (*holds up a finger for silence ... A silence*) A great experience (MORE *keeps silent.*)... A great experience, Thomas.

MORE   Yes, Your Grace.

The music is growing fainter.

HENRY I am a fool.

MORE How so, Your Grace?

HENRY (*a silence, during which the music fades to silence*) ... What else but a fool to live in a Court, in a licentious mob — when I have friends, with gardens.

MORE Your Grace —

HENRY No courtship, no ceremony, Thomas. Be seated. You *are* my friend are you not? (MORE *sits.*)

MORE Your Majesty.

HENRY And thank God I have a friend for my Chancellor. (*Laughing.*) Readier to be friends I trust than he was to be Chancellor.

MORE My own knowledge of my poor abilities —

HENRY I will judge of your abilities, Thomas ... Did you know that Wolsey named you for Chancellor?

MORE Wolsey!

HENRY Aye; before he died. Wolsey named you and Wolsey was no fool.

MORE He was a statesman of incomparable ability, Your Grace.

HENRY Was he? Was he so? (*Rises.*) Then why did he fail me? Be seated — it was villainy then! Yes villainy. I was right to break him; he was all pride, Thomas; a proud man; pride right through. And he failed me! (MORE *opens his mouth.*) He failed me in the one thing that mattered! The one thing that matters, Thomas, then or now. And why? He wanted to be Pope! Yes, he wanted to be the Bishop of Rome. I'll tell you something. Thomas, and you can check this for yourself — it was never merry in England while we had Cardinals amongst us. (*He nods significantly at* MORE *who lowers his eyes.*) But look now — (*walking away*) — I shall never forget the feel of that ... great tiller under my hands ... I took her down to Dogget's Bank, went about and brought her up in Tilbury Roads. A man could sail clean round the world in that ship.

MORE   (*affectionate admiration*) Some men could, Your Grace.

HENRY   (*off-hand*) Touching this matter of my divorce, Thomas; have you thought of it since we last talked?

MORE   Of little else.

HENRY   Then you see your way clear to me?

MORE   That you should put away Queen Catherine, sire? Oh, alas (*thumps table in distress*), as I think of it I see so clearly that I can *not* come with Your Grace that my endeavour is not to think of it at all.

HENRY   Then you have not thought enough! ... (*With real appeal.*) Great God, Thomas, why do you hold out against me in the desire of my heart — the very wick of my heart? —

MORE   (*draws up sleeve, baring his arm*) There is my right arm. (*A practical proposition.*) Take your dagger and saw it from my shoulder, and I will laugh and be thankful, if by that means I can come with Your Grace with a clear conscience.

HENRY   (*uncomfortably pulls at the sleeve*) I know it, Thomas, I know...

MORE   (*rises, formally*) I crave pardon if I offend.

HENRY   (*suspiciously*) Speak then.

MORE   When I took the Great Seal your Majesty promised not to pursue me on this matter.

HENRY   Ha! So I break my word, Master More! No, no, I'm joking ... I joke roughly ... (*Wanders away.*) I often think I'm a rough fellow.... Yes, a rough young fellow. (*Shakes his head indulgently.*) Be seated ... That's a magnolia. We have one like it at Hampton — not so red as that though. Ha — I'm in an excellent frame of mind. (*Glances at the magnolia.*) Beautiful. (*Reasonable, pleasant.*) You must consider, Thomas, that I stand in peril of my soul. It was no marriage; she was my brother's widow. Leviticus: 'Thou shalt not uncover the nakedness of thy brother's wife.' Leviticus, Chapter 18, Verse 16.

MORE   Yes, Your Grace. But Deuteronomy —

HENRY   (*triumphant*) Deuteronomy's ambiguous!

MORE   (*bursting out*) Your Grace, I'm not fit to meddle
        in these matters — to me it seems a matter for the
        Holy See —

HENRY   (*reproving*) Thomas, Thomas, does a man need a
        Pope to tell him when he's sinned? It was a sin,
        Thomas; I admit it; I repent. And God has punished
        me; I have no son ... Son after son she's borne me,
        Thomas, all dead at birth, or dead within the month;
        I never saw the hand of God so clear in anything....
        I have a daughter, she's a good child, a well-set child
        — But I have no son. (*Flares up.*) It is my bounden
        duty to put away the Queen and all the Popes back
        to St Peter shall not come between me and my duty!
        How is it that you cannot see? Everyone else does.

MORE   (*eagerly*) Then why does Your Grace need my poor
        support?

HENRY   Because you are honest. What's more to the purpose,
        you're known to be honest ... There are those like Norfolk
        who follow me because I wear the crown, and there are
        those like Master Cromwell who follow me because they
        are jackals with sharp teeth and I am their lion, and there is
        a mass that follows me because it follows anything that
        moves — and there is you.

MORE   I am sick to think how much I must displease
        Your Grace.

HENRY   No, Thomas, I respect your sincerity. Respect?
        Oh, man it's water in the desert ... How did you
        like our music? That air they played, it had a
        certain — well, tell me what you thought of it.

MORE   (*relieved at this turn; smiling*) Could it have been
        Your Grace's own?

HENRY   (*smiles back*) Discovered! Now I'll never know
        your true opinion. And that's irksome, Thomas,
        for we artists, though we love praise, yet we love
        truth better.

MORE   (*mildly*) Then I will tell Your Grace truly what I thought of
        it.

HENRY   (*a little disconcerted*) Speak then.

MORE   To me it seemed — delightful.

HENRY   Thomas — I chose the right man for Chancellor.

MORE   I must in fairness add that my taste in music is reputedly
        deplorable.

HENRY   Your taste in music is excellent. It exactly coincides
        with my own. Ah music! Music! Send them back
        without me, Thomas; I will live here in Chelsea and
        make music.

MORE   My house is at Your Grace's disposal.

HENRY   Thomas, you understand me; we will stay here together
        and make music.

MORE   Will Your Grace honour my roof at dinner?

HENRY   (*has walked away, blowing moodily on his whistle*) Mm?
        Yes; I expect I'll bellow for you...

MORE   My wife will be more —

HENRY   Yes, yes. (*He turns, his face set.*) Touching this
        other business, mark you, Thomas, I'll have no
        opposition.

MORE   (*sadly*) Your Grace?

HENRY   No opposition I say! No opposition! Your conscience
        is your own affair; but you are my Chancellor! There,
        you have my word — I'll leave you out of it. But I don't
        take it kindly, Thomas, and I'll have no opposition!
        I see how it will be; the Bishops will oppose me. The
        full-fed, hypocritical, 'Princes of the *Church*'! Ha! As
        for the Pope — Am I to burn in Hell because the Bishop
        of Rome with the Emperor's knife to his throat,
        mouths me Deuteronomy? Hypocrites! They're all
        hypocrites! Mind they do not take you in, Thomas!
        Lie low if you will, but I'll brook no opposition —
        no words, no signs, no letters, no pamphlets — mind
        that, Thomas — no writings against me!

MORE   Your Grace is unjust. I am Your Grace's loyal minister.
        If I cannot serve Your Grace in this great matter of the
        Queen —

HENRY   I have no Queen! Catherine is not my wife and no priest
        can make her so, and they that say she is my wife are

not only liars…but Traitors! Mind it, Thomas!

MORE Am I a babbler, Your Grace? (*But his voice is unsteady.*)

HENRY You are stubborn… (*Wooingly.*) If you could come with me, you are the man I would soonest raise — yes, with my own hand.

MORE (*covers his face*) Oh, Your Grace overwhelms me!

A complicated chiming of little bells is heard.

HENRY What's that?

MORE Eight o'clock, Your Grace.

HENRY (*uneasily eyeing* MORE) Oh, lift yourself up, man — have I not promised? (MORE *braces.*) Shall we eat?

MORE If Your Grace pleases. (*Recovering.*) What will Your Grace sing for us? (*They approach the stairs.*)

HENRY Eight o'clock you said? Thomas, the tide will be changing. I was forgetting the tide. I'd better go.

MORE (*gravely*) I'm sorry, Your Grace.

HENRY I must catch the tide or I'll not get back to Richmond till… No, don't come. Tell Norfolk. (*He has his foot on the bottom stair when enter* ALICE *and* STEWARD *above.*) Oh, Lady Alice, I must go. (ALICE *descends, her face serious.*) I want to catch the tide. To tell the truth, Lady Alice, I have forgotten in your haven here how time flows past outside. Affairs call me to court and so I give you my thanks and say Good night.

(*He mounts.*)

MORE}
ALICE} (*bowing*) Good night, Your Grace.

Exit HENRY, *above.*

ALICE What's this? You crossed him.

MORE Somewhat.

ALICE Why?

MORE (*apologetic*) I couldn't find the other way.

ALICE (*angrily*) You're too nice altogether, Thomas!

MORE Woman, mind your house.

ALICE I *am* minding my house!

MORE	(*takes in her anxiety*) Well, Alice. What would you *want* me to do?
ALICE	Be ruled! If you won't rule him, be ruled!
MORE	(*quietly*) I neither could nor would rule my King. (*Pleasantly.*) But there's a little … little, area … where I must rule myself. It's very little — less to him than a tennis court. (*Her face is still full of foreboding: he sighs.*) Look; it was eight o'clock. At eight o'clock, Lady Anne likes to dance.
ALICE	(*relieved*) Oh?
MORE	I think so.
ALICE	(*irritation*) And *you* stand between them!
MORE	I? What stands between them is a sacrament of the Church. I'm less important than you think, Alice.
ALICE	(*appealing*) Thomas, stay friends with him.
MORE	Whatever can be done by smiling, you may rely on me to do.
ALICE	You don't know *how* to flatter.
MORE	I flatter very well! My recipe's beginning to be widely copied. It's the basic syrup with just a soupçon of discreet impudence….
ALICE	(*still uneasy*) I wish he'd eaten here ….
MORE	Yes — we shall be living on that 'simple supper' of yours for a fortnight. (*She won't laugh.*) Alice … (*She won't turn.*) Alice….(*She turns.*) Set your mind at rest — this (*tapping himself*) is not the stuff of which martyrs are made.

Enter above, quickly, ROPER.

ROPER	Sir Thomas!
MORE	(*winces*) Oh, no …!
ALICE	Will Roper, what d'you want?

Enter after ROPER, MARGARET.

MARGARET	William, I told you not to!
ROPER	I'm not easily 'told', Meg.
MARGARET	I *asked* you not to.
ROPER	Meg, I'm full to here! (*Indicates throat.*)
MARGARET	It's not convenient!

ROPER   Must everything be made convenient? I'm not a convenient
man, Meg — I've got an inconvenient conscience!

MARGARET *gestures helplessly to* MORE.

MORE   (*laughs*) Joshua's trumpet. One note on that brass
conscience of yours and my daughter's walls are down.

ROPER   (*descending*) You raised her, sir.

MORE   (*a bit puzzled*) How long have you been here? Are you in
the King's party?

ROPER   No, sir, I am *not* in the King's party! (*Advancing.*) It's of
that I wish to speak to you. My spirit is perturbed.

MORE   (*suppressing a grin*) Is it, Will? Why?

ROPER   I've been offered a seat in the next Parliament. (MORE *looks
up sharply.*) Ought I to take it?

MORE   No ... Well that depends. With your views on Church
Reformation I should have thought you could do yourself a
lot of good in the next Parliament.

ROPER   My views on the Church — I must confess — Since last
we met my views have somewhat modified (MORE
and MARGARET *exchange a smile.*) I modify nothing
concerning the *body* of the Church — the money-
changers in the temple must be scourged from thence
— with a scourge of fire if that is needed! ... But an
attack on the Church herself! No, I see behind that an
attack on God —

MORE   — Roper —

ROPER   The Devil's work!

MORE   — Roper — !

ROPER   To be done by the Devil's ministers!

MORE   For heaven's sake remember my office!

ROPER   Oh, if you stand on your office —

MORE   I don't stand on it, but there are certain things I may not
hear!

ROPER   Sophistication. It is what I was told. The Court has
corrupted you, Sir Thomas; you are not the man you
were; you have learnt to study your 'convenience';
you have learnt to flatter!

MORE	There, Alice; you see? I have a reputation for it.
ALICE	God's Body, young man, if I was the Chancellor I'd have you whipped!
	Enter STEWARD.
STEWARD	Master Rich is here, Sir Thomas.
	RICH *follows him closely.*
RICH	Good evening, sir.
MORE	Ah, Richard?
RICH	Good evening, Lady Alice. (ALICE *nods, noncommittal.*) Lady Margaret.
MARGARET	(*quite friendly but very clear*) Good evening, Master Rich.
	A pause.
MORE	Do you know — ? (*Indicates* ROPER.) William Roper, the younger.
RICH	By reputation, of course.
ROPER	Good evening, Master …
RICH	Rich.
ROPER	(*Recollecting something.*) Oh.
RICH	(*quick and hostile*) You have heard of me?
ROPER	(*shortly*) Yes.
RICH	(*excitedly*) In what connection? I don't know what you can have heard — (*Looks about: hotly.*) I sense that I'm not welcome here! (*He has jumped the gun; they are startled.*)
MORE	(*gently*) Why, Richard, have you done something that should make you not welcome?
RICH	Why, do you suspect me of it?
MORE	I shall begin to.
RICH	(*draws closer to him and speaks hurriedly*) Cromwell is asking questions. About you. About you particularly. (MORE *is unmoved.*) He is continually collecting information about you!
MORE	I know it. (STEWARD *begins to slide out.*) Stay a minute, Matthew.
RICH	(*pointing*) *That's* one of his sources!

MORE   Of course; that's one of my servants.

RICH   (*hurried, low voice again*) Signor Chapuys, the Imperial
                Ambassador —

MORE   — Collects information too. That's one of his functions.

                (*He looks at* RICH *gravely.*)

RICH   (*voice cracking*) You look at me as though I were an
                enemy!

MORE   (*puts out a hand to steady him*) Why, Richard, you're
                shaking.

RICH   I'm adrift. Help me.

MORE   How?

RICH   Employ me.

MORE   No.

RICH   (*desperately*) Employ me!

MORE   No!

RICH   (*moves swiftly to exit; turns there*) I would be steadfast!

MORE   Richard, you couldn't answer for yourself even so far as
                tonight.

                Exit RICH. *All watch him; the others turn to* MORE, *their
                faces alert.*

ROPER   Arrest him.

ALICE   Yes!

MORE   For what?

ALICE   He's dangerous!

ROPER   For libel; he's a spy.

ALICE   He is! Arrest him!

MARGARET   Father, that man's bad.

MORE   There is no law against that.

ROPER   There is! God's law!

MORE   Then God can arrest him.

ROPER   Sophistication upon sophistication!

MORE   No, sheer simplicity. The law, Roper, the law. I know
                what's legal not what's right. And I'll stick to what's legal.

ROPER   Then you set Man's law above God's!

MORE   No, far below; but let me draw your attention to a fact — I'm *not* God. The currents and eddies of right and wrong, which you find such plain-sailing, I can't navigate, I'm no voyager. But in the thickets of the law, oh there I'm a forester. I doubt if there's a man alive who could follow me there, thank God... (*He says this to himself.*)

ALICE   (*exasperated, pointing after* RICH) While you talk, he's gone!

MORE   And go he should if he was the devil himself until he broke the law!

ROPER   So now you'd give the Devil benefit of law!

MORE   Yes. What would you do? Cut a great road through the law to get after the Devil?

ROPER   I'd cut down every law in England to do that!

MORE   (*roused and excited*) Oh? (*Advances on* ROPER.) And when the last law was down, and the Devil turned round on you — where would you hide, Roper, the laws all being flat? (*Leaves him.*) This country's planted thick with laws from coast to coast — Man's laws, not God's — and if you cut them down — and you're just the man to do it — d'you really think you could stand upright in the winds that would blow then? (*Quietly.*) Yes, I'd give the Devil benefit of law, for my own safety's sake.

ROPER   I have long suspected this; this is the golden calf; the law's your god.

MORE   (*wearily*) Oh, Roper, you're a fool, God's my god... (*Rather bitter.*) But I find him rather too (*very bitter*) subtle ... I don't know where he is nor what he wants.

ROPER   My god wants service, to the end and unremitting; nothing else!

MORE   (*dry*) Are you sure that's God? He sounds like Moloch. But indeed it may be God — And whoever hunts for me, Roper, God or Devil, will find me hiding in the thickets of the law! And I'll hide my daughter with me! Not hoist her up the mainmast of your seagoing principles! They put about too nimbly!

Exit MORE. *They all look after him.* MARGARET *touches* ROPER'S *hand.*

MARGARET   Oh, that was harsh.

ROPER   (*turning to her, serious*) What's happened here?

ALICE   (*still with her back to them, her voice strained*) He can't abide a fool, that's all! Be off!

ROPER   (*To* MARGARET) Hide you. Hide you from what?

ALICE   (*turning, near to tears*) He said nothing about hiding me you noticed! I've got too fat to hide I suppose!

MARGARET   You know he meant us both.

ROPER   But from what?

ALICE   I don't know. I don't know if he knows. He's not said one simple, direct word to me since this divorce came up. It's not God who's gone subtle! It's him!

Enter MORE, *a little sheepish. Goes to* ROPER.

MORE   (*kindly*) Roper, that was harsh: your principles are — (*can't resist sending him up*) excellent — the very best quality. (ROPER *bridles. Contrite.*) No truly now, your principles are fine. (*Indicating stairs, to all.*) Look, we must make a start on all that food.

MARGARET   Father, can't you be plain with us?

MORE   (*looks quickly from daughter to wife. Takes* ALICE'S *hand*) I stand on the wrong side of no statute, and no common law. (*Takes* MEG'S *hand too.*) I have not disobeyed my sovereign. I truly believe no man in England is safer than myself. And I want my supper. (*He starts them up the stairs and goes to* ROPER.) We shall need your assistance, Will. There's an excellent Burgundy — if your principles permit.

ROPER   They don't, sir.

MORE   Well, have some water in it.

ROPER   Just the water, sir.

MORE   My poor boy.

ALICE   (*stopping at head of stairs, as one who will be answered*) Why does Cromwell collect information about you?

MORE   I'm a prominent figure. Someone somewhere's collecting information about Cromwell. Now no more shirking; we must make a start. (*Shepherding* ROPER *up the stairs.*) There's a stuffed swan if you please. (ALICE *and* MARGARET *exit above.*) Will, I'd trust *you* with my life. But not your principles. (*They mount the stairs.*) You see, we speak of being anchored to our principles. But if the weather turns nasty you up with an anchor and let it down where there's less wind, and the fishing's better. And 'look' we say 'I'm anchored!' (*Laughing, inviting* ROPER *to laugh with him.*) 'To my principles!'

Exit above, MORE *and* ROPER. *Enter* COMMON MAN *pulling basket. From it he takes an Inn Sign which he hangs on to the alcove. He inspects it.*

COMMON MAN 'The Loyal Subject'… (*to audience*) a pub (*takes from basket and puts on a jacket, cap and napkin*). A publican. (*Places two stools at the table, and mugs and a candle which he lights.*) Oh, he's a deep one that Sir Thomas More… Deep … It takes a lot of education to get a man as deep as that…. (*Straight to audience.*) And a deep nature to begin with too. (*Deadpan.*) The likes of me can hardly be *expected* to follow the processes of a man like that… (*Sly.*) Can we? (*Inspects pub.*) Right, ready. (*Goes right.*) Ready, sir!

Enter CROMWELL, *carrying bottle. Goes to alcove.*

CROMWELL Is this a *good* place for a conspiracy, innkeeper?

PUBLICAN (*woodenly*) You asked for a private room, sir.

CROMWELL (*looking round*) Yes, I want one without too many little dark corners.

PUBLICAN I don't understand you, sir. Just the four corners as you see.

CROMWELL (*sardonic*) You don't understand me.

PUBLICAN That's right, sir.

CROMWELL Do you know who I am?

PUBLICAN (*promptly*) No, sir.

CROMWELL Don't be too tactful, innkeeper.

PUBLICAN I don't understand, sir.

CROMWELL   When the likes of you *are* too tactful, the likes of me begin to wonder who's the fool.

PUBLICAN   I just don't understand you, sir.

CROMWELL   (*puts back his head and laughs silently*) The master statesman of us all. 'I don't understand'. (*Looks at* PUBLICAN *almost with hatred.*) All right. Get out. (*Throws coin. Exit* PUBLICAN. CROMWELL *goes to exit opposite. Calling.*) Come on. (*Enter* RICH. *He glances at bottle in* CROMWELL'S *hand and remains cautiously by the exit.*) Yes, it may be that I am a little intoxicated. (*Leaves* RICH *standing.*) But not with alcohol, with success! And who has a strong head for success? None of us gets enough of it. Except Kings. And they're born drunk.

RICH   Success? What success?

CROMWELL   Guess.

RICH   Collector of Revenues for York.

CROMWELL   (*amused*) You do keep your ear to the ground don't you? No. Better than that.

RICH   High Constable.

CROMWELL   Better than that.

RICH   Better than High Constable?

CROMWELL   Much better. Sir Thomas Paget is — retiring.

RICH   Secretary to the Council!

CROMWELL   'Tis astonishing, isn't it?

RICH   (*hastily*) Oh no — I mean — one sees, it's logical.

CROMWELL   No ceremony, no courtship. Be seated. (RICH *sits.*) As His Majesty would say. (RICH *laughs nervously and involuntarily glances round.*) Yes; see how I trust you.

RICH   Oh, I would never repeat or report a thing like that —

CROMWELL   (*pouring wine*) What kind of thing would you repeat or report?

RICH   Well, nothing said in friendship — may I say 'friendship'?

CROMWELL   If you like. D'you believe that — that you would never repeat or report anything etcetera?

RICH   Why yes!

CROMWELL	No, but seriously.
RICH	Yes!
CROMWELL	(*puts down bottle. Not sinister, but rather as a kindly teacher with a promising pupil*) Rich; seriously.
RICH	(*pauses, then bitterly*) It would depend what I was offered.
CROMWELL	Don't say it just to please me.
RICH	It's true. It would depend what I was offered.
CROMWELL	(*patting his arm*) Everyone knows it; not many people can say it.
RICH	There are *some* things one wouldn't do for anything. Surely.
CROMWELL	Mm — that idea's like these lifelines they have on the embankment: comforting, but you don't expect to have to use them. (*Briskly.*) Well, congratulations!
RICH	(*suspicious*) On what?
CROMWELL	I think you'd make a good Collector of Revenues for York Diocese.
RICH	(*gripping on to himself*) Is it in your gift?
CROMWELL	Effectively.
RICH	(*conscious cynicism*) What do I have to do for it?
CROMWELL	Nothing. (*He lectures, pacing pedantically up and down.*) It isn't like that, Rich. There are no rules. With rewards and penalties — so much wickedness purchases so much worldly prospering — (*He breaks off and stops, suddenly struck.*) Are you sure you're not religious?
RICH	Almost sure.
CROMWELL	Get sure. (*Resumes pacing*) No, it's not like that, it's much more a matter of convenience, administrative convenience. The normal aim of administration is to keep steady this factor of convenience — and Sir Thomas would agree. Now normally when a man wants to change his woman, you let him if it's convenient and prevent him if it's not — normally indeed it's of so little importance that you leave it to the priests. But the constant factor is this element of convenience.

RICH   Whose convenience? (CROMWELL *stops.*)

CROMWELL   Oh ours. But everybody's too. (*Sets off again.*)
              However, in the present instance the man who
              wants to change his woman is our Sovereign Lord,
              Harry, by the Grace of God, the Eighth of that name.
              Which is a quaint way of saying that if he wants to
              change his woman he will. So *that* becomes the
              constant factor. And our job as administrators is
              to make it as convenient as we can. I say 'our' job,
              on the assumption that you'll take this post at York
              I've offered you?

RICH   Yes…yes, yes. (*But he seems gloomy.*)

CROMWELL   (*sits. Sharply*) It's a bad sign when people are depressed by
              their own good fortune.

RICH   (*defensive*) I'm not depressed!

CROMWELL   You look depressed.

RICH   (*hastily buffooning*) I'm lamenting. I've lost my
              innocence.

CROMWELL   You lost that some time ago. If you've only just
              noticed, it can't have been very important to you.

RICH   (*much struck*) That's true! Why that's true, it can't!

CROMWELL   We experience a sense of release do we, Master Rich? An
              unfamiliar freshness in the head, as of open air?

RICH   (*takes wine*) Collector of Revenues isn't bad!

CROMWELL   Not bad for a start. (*He watches* RICH *drink.*) Now our
              present Lord Chancellor — *there's* an innocent man.

RICH   (*puts down glass. Indulgently*) The odd thing is — he *is*.

CROMWELL   (*looks at him with dislike*) Yes, I say he is. (*The light
              tone again.*) The trouble is, his innocence is tangled
              in this proposition that you can't change your woman
              without a divorce, and can't have a divorce unless the
              Pope says so. And although his present Holiness is —
              judged even by the most liberal standards — a strikingly
              corrupt old person, yet he still has this word 'Pope'
              attached to him. And from this quite meaningless
              circumstance I fear some degree of …

RICH   (*pleased, waving his cup*) Administrative inconvenience.

CROMWELL   (*nodding as to a pupil word perfect*) Just so. (*Dead-*

pan.) This goblet that he gave you, how much was it worth? (RICH *puts down cup, looks down. Quite gently.*) Come along. Rich, he gave you a silver goblet. How much did you get for it?

RICH   Fifty shillings.

CROMWELL   Could you take me to the shop?

RICH   Yes.

CROMWELL   Where did he get it? (*No reply.*) It was a gift from a litigant, a woman, wasn't it?

RICH   Yes.

CROMWELL   Which court? Chancery? (*Restrains* RICH *from filling his glass.*) No, don't get drunk. In which court was this litigant's case?

RICH   Court of Requests.

CROMWELL   (*grunts, his face abstracted. Becoming aware of* RICH'S *regard he smiles*) There, that wasn't too painful was it?

RICH   (*laughing a little and a little rueful*) No!

CROMWELL   (*spreading his hands*) That's all there is. And you'll find it easier next time.

RICH   (*looks up briefly, unhappily*) What application do they have, these titbits of information you collect?

CROMWELL   None at all, usually.

RICH   (*stubbornly, not looking up*) But sometimes.

CROMWELL   Well, there *are* these men, you know — 'upright', 'steadfast', men who want themselves to be the constant factor in the situation. Which of course they can't be. The situation rolls forward in any case.

RICH   (*the same*) So what happens?

CROMWELL   (*not liking his tone, coldly*) If they've any sense they get out of its way.

RICH   What if they haven't any sense?

CROMWELL   (*the same*) What none at all? Well, then they're only fit for Heaven. But Sir Thomas has plenty of sense; he could be frightened.

RICH (*looks up, his face nasty*) Don't forget he's an innocent, Master Cromwell.

CROMWELL I think we'll finish there for tonight. (*Rising.*) After all, he *is* the Lord Chancellor. (*Going.*)

RICH You wouldn't find him easy to frighten! (*Calls after him.*) You've mistaken your man this time! He doesn't know how to be frightened!

CROMWELL (*returning.* RICH *rises at his approach*) Doesn't know how to be frightened? Why, then he never put his hand in a candle... Did he? (*And seizing* RICH *by the wrist he holds his hand in the candle flame.*)

RICH (*screeches and darts back, hugging his hand in his armpit, regarding* CROMWELL *with horror*) You enjoyed that! (CROMWELL'S *downturned face is amazed. Triumphantly.*) You enjoyed it!

CURTAIN

ACT TWO

*The scene is as for start of Act One. When the curtain
rises the stage is in darkness save for a spot, front stage,
in which stands the* COMMON MAN. *He carries the book, a
place marked by his finger, and wears his spectacles.*

COMMON MAN
The interval started early in the year 1530 and it's now the
middle of May 1532. (*Explanatory.*) Two years. During that
time a lot of water's flowed under the bridge and among
the things that have come floating along on it is ... (*Reads.*)
'The Church of England, that finest flower of our Island
genius for compromise; that system, peculiar to these
shores, which deflects the torrents of religious passion
down the canals of moderation.' That's very well put.
(*Returns to book, approvingly.*) 'Typically, this great effect
was achieved not by bloodshed but by simple Act of
Parliament. Only an unhappy few were found to set
themselves against the current of their times, and in so
doing to court disaster. For we are dealing with an age less
fastidious than our own. Imprisonment without trial, and
even examination under torture, were common practice.'

Lights rise to show MORE, *seated, and* ROPER, *standing.
Exit* COMMON MAN. ROPER *is dressed in black and wears
a cross. He commences to walk up and down, watched
by* MORE.

A pause.

MORE
Must you wear those clothes, Will?

ROPER
Yes, I must.

MORE
Why?

ROPER
The time has come for decent men to declare their
allegiance!

MORE	And what allegiance are those designed to express?
ROPER	My allegiance to the Church.
MORE	Well, you *look* like a Spaniard.
ROPER	All credit to Spain then!
MORE	You wouldn't last six months in Spain. You'd have been burned alive in Spain, during your heretic period.
ROPER	I suppose you have the right to remind me of it. (*Points accusingly.*) That chain of office that *you* wear is a degradation.
MORE	(*glances down at it*) I've told you. If the bishops in Convocation submitted this morning, I'll take it off.... It's no degradation. Great men have worn this.
ROPER	When d'you expect to hear from Canterbury?
MORE	About now. The Archbishop promised me an immediate message.
ROPER	(*recommences pacing*) I don't see what difference Convocation can make. The Church is already a wing of the Palace is it not? The King is already its 'Supreme Head'! Is he not?
MORE	No.
ROPER	(*is startled*) You are denying the Act of Supremacy!
MORE	No, I'm not; the Act states that the King —
ROPER	— is Supreme Head of the Church in England.
MORE	Supreme Head of the Church in England — (*Underlining the words*) 'so far as the law of God allows.' How far the law of God does allow it remains a matter of opinion, since the Act doesn't state it.
ROPER	A legal quibble.
MORE	Call it what you like, it's there, thank God.
ROPER	Very well: in your opinion how far does the law of God allow this?
MORE	I'll keep my opinion to myself, Will.
ROPER	Yes? I'll tell you mine — !
MORE	Don't! If your opinion's what I think it is, it's High Treason, Roper!

Enter MARGARET *above, unseen.*

	Will, you remember you've a wife now! And may have children!
MARGARET	Why must he remember that?
ROPER	To keep myself 'discreet'.
MARGARET	(*smiling*) Then I'd rather you forgot it.
MORE	(*unsmiling*) You are either idiots, or children.
	Enter CHAPUYS *above.*
CHAPUYS	Or saints, my lord! (*Very sonorous.*)
MARGARET	Oh, Father, Signor Chapuys has come to see you.
MORE	(*rising*) Your Excellency.
CHAPUYS	(*strikes pose with* MARGARET *and* ROPER) Or saints, my lord; or saints.
MORE	(*grins maliciously at* ROPER) That's it of course — saints! Roper — turn your head a bit — yes, I think I do detect, a faint radiance. (*Reproachful.*) You should have told us, Will.
CHAPUYS	Come come, my lord; you too at this time are not free from some suspicion of saintliness.
MORE	(*quietly*) I don't like the sound of that. Your Excellency. What do you require of *me?* What, Your Excellency?
CHAPUYS	(*awkward beneath his sudden keen regard*) May I not come simply, to pay my respects to the English Socrates — as I see your angelic friend Erasmus calls you.
MORE	(*wrinkles nose*) Yes, I'll think of something presently to call Erasmus. (*Checks.*) Socrates! I've no taste for hemlock, Your Excellency, if that's what you require.
CHAPUYS	(*display of horror*) Heaven forbid!
MORE	(*dryly*) Amen.
CHAPUYS	(*spreads hands*) Must I require anything? (*Sonorous.*) After all, we are brothers in Christ, you and I!
MORE	A characteristic we share with the rest of humanity. You live in Cheapside, Signor? To make contact with a brother in Christ you have only to open your window and empty a chamberpot. There was no need to come to Chelsea. (CHAPUYS *titters nervously. Coldly.*) William. The Imperial Ambassador is here on business. Would you mind?

ROPER *and* MARGARET *going.*

CHAPUYS   (*rising, unreal protestations*) Oh no! I protest!

MORE   He is clearly here on business.

CHAPUYS   (*the same*) No; but really, I protest! (*It is no more than
token: when* ROPER *and* MARGARET *reach head of stairs he
calls*) Dominus vobiscum filii mei!

ROPER   (*pompous*) Et cum spiritu tuo, excellencis!

Exit ROPER *and* MARGARET.

CHAPUYS   (*approaching* MORE, *thrillingly*) And how much longer shall
we hear that holy language in these shores?

MORE   (*alert, poker-faced*) 'Tisn't 'holy', Your Excellency; just old.

CHAPUYS *sits with the air of one coming to brass tacks.*

CHAPUYS   My Lord, I cannot believe you will allow yourself to be
associated with the recent actions of King Henry! In
respect of Queen Catherine.

MORE   Subjects are associated with the actions of Kings
willy-nilly.

CHAPUYS   The Lord Chancellor is not an ordinary subject. He bears
responsibility (*he lets the word sink in*: MORE *shifts*) for
what is done.

MORE   (*agitation begins to show through*) Have you considered
that what has been done badly, might have been done
worse, with a different Chancellor?

CHAPUYS   (*mounting confidence, as* MORE'S *attention is caught*)
Believe me, Sir Thomas, your influence in these policies
has been much searched for, and where it has been found
it has been praised — *but* ... There comes a point, does
there not? ...

MORE   Yes. (*Agitated.*) There does come such a point.

CHAPUYS   When the sufferings of one unfortunate lady swell to an
open attack on the religion of an entire country that point
has been passed. Beyond that point, Sir Thomas, one is not
merely 'compromised,' one is in truth corrupted.

MORE   (*stares at him*) What do you want?

CHAPUYS Rumour has it that if the Church in Convocation has submitted to the King, you will resign.

MORE (*looks down and regains composure*) I see. (*Suave.*) Supposing rumour to be right. Would you approve of that?

CHAPUYS Approve, applaud, admire.

MORE (*still looking down*) Why?

CHAPUYS Because it would show one man — and that man known to be temperate — unable to go further with this wickedness.

MORE (*the same*) And that man known to be Chancellor of England too.

CHAPUYS Believe me, my lord, such a signal would be seen —

MORE (*the same*) 'Signal'?

CHAPUYS Yes, my lord; it would be seen and understood.

MORE (*the same, and now positively silky*) By whom?

CHAPUYS By half of your fellow countrymen! (*Now* MORE *looks up sharply.*) Sir Thomas, I have just returned from Yorkshire and Northumberland, where I have made a tour.

MORE (*softly*) Have you indeed?

CHAPUYS Things are very different there, my lord. There they are ready.

MORE For what?

CHAPUYS Resistance!

Enter ROPER, *above, excited.*

ROPER Sir Thomas — ! (MORE *looks up angrily.*) Excuse me, sir — (*Indicates off.*) His Grace the Duke of Norfolk — (MORE *and* CHAPUYS *rise.* ROPER *excitedly descends.*) It's all over, sir, they've —

Enter NORFOLK *above,* ALICE *and* MARGARET, *below.*

NORFOLK One moment, Roper, I'll do this! Thomas — (*Sees* CHAPUYS.) Oh. (*He stares at* CHAPUYS, *hostile.*)

CHAPUYS I was on the point of leaving, Your Grace. Just a personal call. I have been trying … er to borrow a book — but without success — you're sure you have no copy, my lord? Then I'll leave you. (*Bowing.*) Gentlemen, ladies.

(*Going, up stairs. Stops unseen as* ROPER *speaks.*)

ROPER   Sir Thomas —

NORFOLK   I'll do it, Roper! Convocation's knuckled under, Thomas. They're to pay a fine of a hundred thousand pounds. And ... we've severed the connection with Rome.

MORE   (*smiling bitterly*) 'The connection with Rome' is nice. (*Bitter.*) 'The connection with Rome.' Did *anyone* resist?

NORFOLK   Bishop Fisher.

MORE   Lovely man. (NORFOLK *shrugs.*)

ROPER   (*looking at* MORE) Your Grace, this is quite certain is it?

NORFOLK   Yes. (MORE *puts his hand to his chain.* CHAPUYS *exits. All turn.*) Funny company, Thomas?

MORE   It's quite unintentional. He doesn't mean to be funny. (*Fumbles with chain.*) Help me with this.

NORFOLK   Not I.

ROPER   (*takes a step forward. Then, subdued*) Shall I, sir?

MORE   No thank you, Will. Alice?

ALICE   Hell's fire — God's blood and body *no!* Sun and moon, Master More, you're taken for a wise man! Is this wisdom — to betray your ability, abandon practice, forget your station and your duty to your kin and behave like a printed book!

MORE   (*listens gravely: then*) Margaret, will you?

MARGARET   If you want.

MORE   There's my clever girl. (*She takes it from his neck.*)

NORFOLK   Well, Thomas, why? Make me understand — because I'll tell you now, from where I stand, this looks like cowardice!

MORE   (*excited and angry*) All right I will — this isn't 'Reformation'; this is war against the Church! ... (*Indignant.*) Our King, Norfolk, has declared war on the Pope — because the Pope will not declare that our Queen is not his wife.

NORFOLK   And is she?

MORE   (*cunning*) I'll answer that question for one person only, the King. Aye, and that in private too.

NORFOLK	(*contemptuous*) Man, you're cautious.
MORE	Yes, cautious. I'm not one of your hawks.
NORFOLK	(*walks away and turns*) All right — we're at war with the Pope! The Pope's a Prince, isn't he?
MORE	He is.
NORFOLK	And a bad one?
MORE	Bad enough. But the theory is that he's also the Vicar of God, the descendant of St Peter, our only link with Christ.
NORFOLK	(*sneer*) A tenuous link.
MORE	Oh, tenuous indeed.
NORFOLK	(*to the others*) Does this make sense? (*No reply; they look at* MORE.) You'll forfeit all you've got — which includes the respect of your country — for a theory?
MORE	(*hotly*) The Apostolic Succession of the Pope is — (*Stops: interested*) ... Why, it's a theory yes; you can't see it, can't touch it, it's a theory. (*To* NORFOLK, *very rapid but calm.*) But what matters to me is not whether it's true or not but that I believe it to be true, or rather not that I *believe* it, but that *I* believe it ... I trust I make myself obscure?
NORFOLK	Perfectly.
MORE	That's good. Obscurity's what I have need of now.
NORFOLK	Man, you're sick. This isn't Spain you know.
MORE	(*looks at him; takes him aside: lowered voice*) Have I your word, that what we say here is between us and has no existence beyond these walls?
NORFOLK	(*impatient*) Very well.
MORE	(*almost whispering*) And if the King should command you to repeat what I have said?
NORFOLK	I should keep my word to you!
MORE	Then what has become of your oath of obedience to the King?
NORFOLK	(*indignant*) You lay traps for me!
MORE	(*now grown calm*) No, I show you the times.
NORFOLK	Why do you insult me with these lawyer's tricks?
MORE	Because I am afraid.

NORFOLK	And here's your answer. The King accepts your resignation very sadly; he is mindful of your goodness and past loyalty and in any matter concerning your honour and welfare he will be your good lord. So much for your fear.
MORE	(*flatly*) You will convey my humble gratitude.
NORFOLK	I will. Good day, Alice (*Going.*) I'd rather deal with you than your husband.
MORE	(*complete change of tone; briskly professional*) Oh, Howard! (*Goes to him.*) Signor Chapuys tells me he's just made a 'tour' of the North Country. He thinks we shall have trouble there. So do I.
NORFOLK	(*stolid*) Yes? What kind of trouble?
MORE	The Church — the old Church, not the new Church — is very strong up there. I'm serious, Howard, keep an eye on the Border, this next year; and bear in mind the Old Alliance.
NORFOLK	(*looks at him*) We will. We do... As for the Dago, Thomas, it'll perhaps relieve your mind to know that one of Secretary Cromwell's agents made the tour with him.
MORE	Oh. (*Flash of jealousy.*) Of course if Master Cromwell has matters in hand —
NORFOLK	— He has.
MORE	Yes, I can imagine.
NORFOLK	But thanks for the information. (*Going.*) It's good to know you still have ... some vestige of patriotism.
MORE	(*anger*) That's a remarkably stupid observation, Norfolk!

Exit NORFOLK.

ALICE	So there's an end of you. What will you do now — sit by the fire and make goslings in the ash?
MORE	Not at all, Alice, I expect I'll write a bit. (*He woos them with unhappy cheerfulness.*) I'll write, I'll read, I'll think. I think I'll learn to fish! I'll play with my grandchildren — when son Roper's done his duty. (*Eager.*) Alice, shall I teach you to read?

ALICE   No, by God!

MORE   … Son Roper, *you're* pleased with me I hope?

ROPER   (*goes to him: moved*) Sir, you've made a noble
gesture.

MORE   (*blankly*) A gesture? (*Eager.*) It wasn't possible to
continue, Will. I was not *able* to continue. I would
have if I could! I make no gesture! (*Apprehensive,
looks after* NORFOLK.) My God, I hope it's understood
I make no gesture! (*Turns back to them.*) — Alice, you
don't think I would do this to you for a gesture! *That's*
a gesture! (*Thumbs his nose.*) *That's* a gesture! (*Jerks
up two fingers.*) I'm no street acrobat to make gestures!
I'm practical!

ROPER   You belittle yourself, sir, this was not practical; (*resonant*)
this was moral!

MORE   Oh now I understand you, Will. Morality's *not* practical.
Morality's a gesture. A complicated gesture learned
from books — that's what you say, Alice, isn't it? … And
you, Meg?

MARGARET   It *is*, for most of us, Father.

MORE   Oh no, if you're going to plead humility — ! Oh, you're
cruel. I have a cruel family.

ALICE   Yes, you can fit the cap on anyone you want, I know that
well enough. If there's cruelty in this house, I know where
to look for it.

MARGARET   No, Mother — !

ALICE   Oh, you'd walk on the bottom of the sea and think
yourself a crab if he suggested it! (*To* ROPER.) And you!
You'd dance him to the Tower — You'd dance him to
the block! Like David with a harp! Scattering hymn-
books in his path! (*To* MORE.) Poor silly man, d'you
think they'll *leave* you here to learn to fish?

MORE   (*straight at her*) If we govern our tongues they
will! … Look, I have a word to say about that. I have
made no statement. I've resigned, that's *all*. On the
King's Supremacy, the King's divorce which he'll
now grant himself, the marriage he'll then make —
have you heard me make a statement?

ALICE   No — and if I'm to lose my rank and fall to house-
         keeping I want to know the reason; so make a
         statement now.

MORE   No — (ALICE *exhibits indignation*) — Alice, it's a point of
         law! Accept it from me, Alice, that in silence is my safety
         under the law, but my silence must be absolute, it must
         extend to you.

ALICE   In short you don't trust us!

MORE   (*impatient*) Look — (*advances on her*) I'm the Lord
         Chief Justice, I'm Cromwell, I'm the King's Head Jailer
         — and I take your hand (*does so*) and I clamp it on the
         Bible, on the Blessed Cross (*clamps her hand on his
         closed fist*) and I say: 'Woman, has your husband
         made a statement on these matters?' Now — on peril
         of your soul remember — what's your answer?

ALICE   No.

MORE   And so it must remain. (*He looks round on their
         grave faces.*) Oh, it's only a life-line, we shan't have
         to use it but it's comforting to have. No, no, when
         they find I'm silent they'll ask nothing better than to
         leave me silent; you'll see.

         Enter STEWARD.

STEWARD Sir, the household's in the kitchen. They want to know
         what's happened.

MORE   Oh. Yes. We must speak to them. Alice, they'll mostly have
         to go, my dear. (*To* STEWARD.) But not before we've found
         them places.

ALICE   We can't find places for them all!

MORE   Yes, we can; yes, we can. Tell them so.

ALICE   God's death it comes on us quickly...

         Exit ALICE, MARGARET *and* ROPER.

MORE   What about you, Matthew? It'll be a smaller house-
         hold now, and for you I'm afraid, a smaller wage. Will
         you stay?

STEWARD Don't see how I could then, sir.

MORE   You're a single man.

STEWARD (*awkward*) Well, yes, sir, but I mean I've got my own —

MORE (*quickly*) Quite right, why should you? ... I shall miss you, Matthew.

STEWARD (*man to man jocosity*) No-o-o. You never had much time for *me,* sir. You see through *me,* sir, I know that. (*He almost winks.*)

MORE (*gently insists*) I shall miss you, Matthew; I shall miss you.

Exit MORE. STEWARD *snatches off hat and hurls it to the floor.*

STEWARD Now, damn me isn't that them all over! (*He broods, face downturned.*) Miss — ?...He — ...Miss — ?... *Miss* me?...What's *in* me for *him* to miss...? (*Suddenly he cries out like one who sees a danger at his very feet.*) Wo-AH! (*Chuckling.*) We-e-eyup! (*To audience.*) I nearly fell for it. (*Walks away.*) 'Matthew, will you kindly take a cut in your wages?' 'No, Sir Thomas, I will not.' That's it and (*fiercely*) that's all of it! (*Falls to thought again. Resentfully.*) All right so he's down on his luck! I'm sorry. I don't mind saying that: I'm sorry! Bad luck! If I'd any good luck to spare he could have some. I wish we could *all* have good luck, *all* the time! I wish we had wings! I wish rainwater was beer! But it isn't!...And what with not having wings but walking — on two flat feet; and good luck and bad luck being just exactly even stevens; and rain being water — don't you complicate the job by putting things in me for me to miss! (*He takes off* STEWARD'S *coat, picks up his hat: draws the curtain to alcove. Chuckling.*) I did you know. I nearly fell for it.

Exit COMMON MAN. NORFOLK *and* CROMWELL *enter to alcove.*

NORFOLK But he makes no noise, Mr Secretary; he's silent, why not leave him silent?

CROMWELL (*patiently*) Not being a man of letters, Your Grace, you perhaps don't realise the extent of his reputation. This

'silence' of his is bellowing up and down Europe! Now
may I recapitulate: He reported the Ambassador's
conversation to you, informed on the Ambassador's tour of
the North-country, warned against a possible rebellion
there.

NORFOLK He did!

CROMWELL We may say then, that he showed himself hostile to the
hopes of Spain.

NORFOLK That's what I *say!*

CROMWELL (*patiently*) Bear with me, Your Grace. Now if he opposes
Spain, he supports us. Well, surely that follows?
(*Sarcastically.*) Or do you see some third alternative?

NORFOLK No, no, that's the line-up all right. And I may say Thomas
More —

CROMWELL Thomas More will line up on the right side.

NORFOLK Yes! Crank he may be, traitor he is not.

CROMWELL (*spreading his hands*) And with a little pressure, he can be
got to say so. And that's all we need — a brief declaration of
his loyalty to the present administration.

NORFOLK I still say let sleeping dogs lie.

CROMWELL (*heavily*) The King does not agree with you.

NORFOLK (*glances at him; flickers, but then rallies*) What kind of
'pressure' d'you think you can bring to bear?

CROMWELL I have evidence that Sir Thomas, during the period of his
judicature, accepted bribes.

NORFOLK (*incredulous*) What! Goddammit he was the only
judge since Cato who *didn't* accept bribes! When
was there last a Chancellor whose posessions after
three years in office totalled one hundred pounds and
a gold chain.

CROMWELL (*rings hand-bell and calls*) Richard! It is, as you imply,
common practice, but a practice may be common and
remain an offence; this offence could send a man to the
Tower.

NORFOLK (*contemptuous*) I don't believe it.

Enter RICH *and* A WOMAN. *He motions her to remain, and*

approaches the table, where CROMWELL *indicates a seat. He has acquired self-importance.*

CROMWELL   Ah, Richard. You know His Grace of course.

RICH   (*respectful affability*) Indeed yes, we're *old* friends.

NORFOLK   (*savage snub*) Used to look after my books or something, didn't you?

CROMWELL   (*clicks his fingers at* WOMAN) Come here. This woman's name is Catherine Anger; she comes from Lincoln. And she put a case in the Court of Requests in — (*Consults paper.*)

WOMAN   A property case, it was.

CROMWELL   Be quiet. A property case in the Court of Requests in April 1526.

WOMAN   And got a wicked false judgement!

CROMWELL   And got an impeccably correct judgement from our friend Sir Thomas.

WOMAN   No, sir, it was not!

CROMWELL   We're not concerned with the judgement but the gift you gave the judge. Tell this gentleman about that. The judgement for what it's worth was the right one.

WOMAN   No, sir! (CROMWELL *looks at her: she hastily addresses* NORFOLK.) I sent him a cup, sir; an Italian silver cup I bought in Lincoln for a hundred shillings.

NORFOLK   Did Sir Thomas accept this cup?

WOMAN   I sent it.

CROMWELL   He did accept it, we can corroborate that. You can go. (*She opens her mouth.*) Go!

Exit WOMAN.

NORFOLK   (*scornful*) Is that your witness?

CROMWELL   No; by an odd coincidence this cup later came into the hands of Master Rich here.

NORFOLK   How?

RICH   He gave it to me.

NORFOLK   (*brutal*) Can you corroborate that?

CROMWELL   I have a fellow outside who can; he was More's

steward at that time. Shall I call him?

NORFOLK   Don't bother, I know him. When did Thomas give you this
            thing?

RICH   I don't exactly remember.

NORFOLK   Well, make an effort. Wait! I can tell you! I can tell
            you — it was that Spring — it was that night we were
            there together. You had a cup with you when we left;
            was that it?

            RICH *looks to* CROMWELL *for guidance but gets none.*

RICH   It may have been.

NORFOLK   Did he often give you cups?

RICH   I don't suppose so, Your Grace.

NORFOLK   That was it then. (*New realisation.*) And it was
            April! The April of 26. The very month that cow
            first put her case before him! (*Triumphant.*) In
            other words the moment he knew it was a bribe,
            he got rid of it.

CROMWELL   (*nodding judicially*) The facts will bear that interpretation
            I suppose.

NORFOLK   Oh, this is a horse that won't run, Master Secretary.

CROMWELL   Just a trial canter, Your Grace. We'll find something
            better.

NORFOLK   (*between bullying and plea*) Look here, Cromwell, I want
            no part of this.

CROMWELL   You have no choice.

NORFOLK   What's that you say?

CROMWELL   The King particularly wishes you to be active in the matter.

NORFOLK   (*winded*) He has not told me that.

CROMWELL   (*politely*) Indeed? He told me.

NORFOLK   But *why?*

CROMWELL   We feel that, since you are known to have been a friend of
            More's, your participation will show that there is nothing
            in the nature of a 'persecution', but only the strict
            processes of law. As indeed you've just demonstrated. I'll
            tell the King of your loyalty to your friend. If you like, I'll
            tell him that you 'want no part of it', too.

NORFOLK   (*furious*) Are you threatening me, Cromwell?

CROMWELL   My *dear* Norfolk ... This isn't Spain.

           NORFOLK *stares,* **turns abruptly and exits.** CROMWELL *turns a look of glacial coldness upon* RICH.

RICH   I'm sorry, Secretary, I'd forgotten he was there that night.

CROMWELL   (*scrutinises him dispassionately, then*) You must try to remember these things.

RICH   Secretary, I'm sincerely — !

CROMWELL   (*dismisses the topic with a wave and turns to look after* NORFOLK) Not such a fool as he looks, the Duke.

RICH   (*Civil Service simper*) That would hardly be possible, Secretary.

CROMWELL   (*straightening papers, briskly*) Sir Thomas is going to be a slippery fish, Richard; we need a net with a finer mesh.

RICH   Yes, Secretary?

CROMWELL   We'll weave one for him shall we, you and I?

RICH   (*uncertain*) I'm only anxious to do what is correct, Secretary.

CROMWELL   (*smiling at him*) Yes, Richard, I know. (*Straightfaced.*) You're absolutely right, it must be done by law. It's just a matter of finding the right law. Or making one. Bring my papers, will you?

           Exit CROMWELL. *Enter* STEWARD.

STEWARD   Could we have a word now, sir?

RICH   We don't require you after all, Matthew.

STEWARD   No, sir, but about ...

RICH   Oh yes... Well, I begin to need a steward, certainly; my household is expanding....(*Sharply.*) But as I remember, Matthew, your attitude to me was sometimes — disrespectful! (*The last word is shrill.*)

STEWARD   (*with humble dignity*) Oh. Oh, I must contradict you there, sir; that's your imagination. In those days, sir, you still had your way to make. And a gentleman in that position often imagines these things. Then when he's risen to his proper level, sir, he stops thinking about it. (*As one offering tangible proof.*) Well — I don't think you find people 'disrespectful' nowadays, do you, sir?

RICH There may be something in that. Bring my papers. (*Going, turns at exit and anxiously scans* STEWARD'S *face for signs of impudence.*) I'll permit no breath of insolence!

STEWARD (*the very idea is shocking*) I should hope not, sir. (*Exit* RICH.) Oh, I can manage this one! He's just my size! (*Lighting changes so that the set looks drab and chilly.*) Sir Thomas More's again gone down a bit.

Exit COMMON MAN.

Enter, side, CHAPUYS *and* ATTENDANT, *cloaked. Above,* ALICE, *wearing big coarse apron over her dress.*

ALICE My husband is coming down, Your Excellency.

CHAPUYS Thank you, madam.

ALICE And I beg you to be gone before he does!

CHAPUYS (*patiently*) Madam, I have a Royal Commission to perform.

ALICE Aye. You said so. (*Exit* ALICE.)

CHAPUYS For sheer barbarity, commend me to a good-hearted Englishwoman of a certain class... (*Wraps cloak about him.*)

ATTENDANT It's very cold, Excellency.

CHAPUYS I remember when these rooms were warm enough.

ATTENDANT (*looking about*) 'Thus it is to incur the enmity of a Prince.'

CHAPUYS A heretic Prince. (*Looking about.*) Yes, Sir Thomas is a good man.

ATTENDANT Yes, Excellency, I like Sir Thomas very much.

CHAPUYS Carefully, carefully.

ATTENDANT It's uncomfortable dealing with him, isn't it?

CHAPUYS Goodness presents its own difficulties. Attend and learn now.

ATTENDANT Excellency?

CHAPUYS	Well?
ATTENDANT	Excellency, is he really *for* us?
CHAPUYS	(*testy*) He's opposed to Cromwell. He's shown that, I think?
ATTENDANT	Yes, Excellency, but —
CAPUYS	If he's opposed to Cromwell, he's for us. There's no third alternative.
ATTENDANT	I suppose not, Excellency.
CHAPUYS	I wish your mother had chosen some other career for you; you've no political sense whatever. Sh!

Enter MORE. *His clothes match the atmosphere of the room and he moves rather more deliberately than before.*

MORE	(*descending*) Is this another 'personal' visit, Chapuys, or is it official?
CHAPUYS	It falls between the two, Sir Thomas.
MORE	(*reaching the bottom of stairs*) Official then.
CHAPUYS	No, I have a personal letter for you.
MORE	From whom?
CHAPUYS	From King Charles! (MORE *puts hands behind back.*) You will take it?
MORE	I will not lay a finger on it.
CHAPUYS	It is in no way an affair of State. It expresses my master's admiration for the stand which you and Bishop Fisher of Rochester have taken over the so-called divorce of Queen Catherine.
MORE	I have taken no stand!
CHAPUYS	But your views, Sir Thomas, are well known —
MORE	My views are much guessed at. (*Irritably.*) Oh come, sir, could you undertake to convince (*grimly*) King Harry that this letter is 'in no way an affair of State'?
CHAPUYS	My dear Sir Thomas, I have taken extreme precautions. I came here very much incognito. (*Self-indulgent chuckle.*) Very nearly in disguise.
MORE	You misunderstand me. It is not a matter of your precautions but my duty; which would be to take this letter

immediately to the King.

CHAPUYS (*flabbergasted*) But, Sir Thomas, your views —

MORE — Are well known you say. It seems my loyalty is less so.

Enter MARGARET *bearing before her a huge bundle of bracken.*

MARGARET Look, Father! (*Dumps it.*) Will's getting more.

MORE Oh, well done! (*Not whimsy; they're cold and their interest in fuel is serious.*) Is it dry? (*Feels it expertly.*) Oh it is. (*Sees* CHAPUYS *staring; laughs.*) It's bracken, Your Excellency. We burn it. (*Enter* ALICE.) Alice, look at this. (*The bracken.*)

ALICE (*Eyeing* CHAPUYS) Aye.

MORE (*Crossing to* CHAPUYS) May I — ? (*Takes letter to* ALICE *and* MARGARET.) This is a letter from King Charles; I want you to see it's not been opened. I have declined it. You see the seal has not been broken? (*Returning it to* CHAPUYS.) I wish I could ask you to stay, Your Excellency — the bracken fire is a luxury.

CHAPUYS (*cold smile*) One I must forego. (*Aside to* ATTENDANT.) Come. (*Crosses to exit, pauses.*) May I say I am sure my master's admiration will not be diminished. (*Bows.*)

MORE I am gratified. (*Bows, women curtsey.*)

CHAPUYS (*aside to* ATTENDANT) The man's utterly unreliable!

Exit CHAPUYS *and* ATTENDANT.

ALICE (*after a little silence kicks the bracken*) 'Luxury!' (*She sits wearily on the bundle.*)

MORE Well, it's a luxury while it lasts... There's not much sport in it for you, is there? ... (*She neither answers nor looks at him from the depths of her fatigue. After a moment's hesitation he braces himself.*) Alice, the money from the Bishops. I wish — oh heaven how I wish I could take it! But I can't.

ALICE (*as one who has ceased to expect anything*) I didn't think you would.

MORE (*reproachful*) Alice, there *are* reasons.

ALICE We couldn't come so deep into your confidence as to *know* these reasons why a man in poverty can't take four thousand pounds?

MORE	(*gently but very firm*) Alice, this isn't poverty.
ALICE	D'you know what we shall eat tonight?
MORE	(*trying for a smile*) Yes, parsnips.
ALICE	Yes, parsnips and stinking mutton! (*Straight at him.*) For a knight's lady!
MORE	(*pleading*) But at the worst, we could be beggars, and still keep company, and be merry together!
ALICE	(*bitterly*) Merry!
MORE	(*sternly*) Aye, merry!
MARGARET	(*her arm about her mother's waist*) I think you should take that money.
MORE	Oh, don't you see? (*Sits by them.*) If I'm paid by the Church for my writings —
ALICE	This had nothing to do with your writings! This was charity pure and simple! Collected from the clergy high and low!
MORE	It would *appear* as payment.
ALICE	You're not a man who deals in appearances!
MORE	(*fervent*) Oh, am I not though... (*Calmly.*) If the King takes this matter any further, with me or with the Church, it will be very bad, if I even appear to have been in the pay of the Church.
ALICE	(*sharply*) Bad?
MORE	If you will have it, dangerous. (*He gets up.*)
MARGARET	But you don't write against the King.
MORE	I write! And that's enough in times like these!
ALICE	You said there *was* no danger!
MORE	I don't think there is! And I don't want there to be!

Enter ROPER *carrying sickle.*

ROPER	(*steadily*) There's a gentleman here from Hampton Court. You are to go before Secretary Cromwell. To answer certain charges. (ALICE *and* MARGARET, *appalled, turn to* MORE.)
MORE	(*after a silence, rubs his nose*) Well, that's all right. We expected that. (*Not very convincing.*) When?

ROPER	Now. (ALICE *exhibits distress.*)
MORE	That means nothing, Alice; that's just technique… Well, I suppose 'now' means now.

Lighting change commences, darkness gathering on the others, leaving MORE *isolated in the light, out of which he answers them in the shadows.*

MARGARET	Can I come with you?
MORE	Why? No. I'll be back for dinner. I'll bring Cromwell to dinner, shall I? It'd serve him right.
MARGARET	Oh, Father, don't be witty!
MORE	Why not? Wit's what's in question.
ROPER	(*quietly*) While we are witty, the Devil may enter us unawares.
MORE	He's not the Devil, son Roper, he's a lawyer! And my case is watertight!
ALICE	They say he's a very nimble lawyer.
MORE	What, Cromwell? Pooh, he's a pragmatist — and that's the only resemblance he has to the Devil, son Roper; a pragmatist, the merest plumber.

Exit ALICE, MARGARET, ROPER, *in darkness.*

Lights come up. Enter CROMWELL, *bustling, carrying file of papers.*

CROMWELL	I'm sorry to invite you here at such short notice, Sir Thomas; good of you to come. (*Draws back curtain from alcove, revealing* RICH *seated at table, with writing materials.*) Will you take a seat? I think you know Master Rich?
MORE	Indeed yes, we're old friends. That's a nice gown you have, Richard.
CROMWELL	Master Rich will make a record of our conversation.
MORE	Good of you to tell me, Master Secretary.
CROMWELL	(*laughs appreciatively. Then*) Believe me, Sir Thomas — no, that's asking too much — but let me tell you all the same, you have no more sincere admirer than myself.

(RICH *begins to scribble.*) Not yet, Rich, not yet. (*Invites* MORE *to join him in laughing at* RICH.)

MORE   If I might hear the charges?

CROMWELL   Charges?

MORE   I understand there are certain charges.

CROMWELL   Some ambiguities of behaviour I should like to clarify — hardly 'charges'.

MORE   Make a note of that will you, Master Rich? There are no charges.

CROMWELL   (*laughing and shaking head*) Sir Thomas, Sir Thomas … You know it amazes me that you, who were once so effective *in* the world, and are now so *much* retired from it, should be opposing yourself to the whole movement of the times? (*He ends on a note of interrogation.*)

MORE   (*nods*) It amazes me too.

CROMWELL   (*picks up and drops paper. Sadly*) The King is not pleased with you.

MORE   I am grieved.

CROMWELL   Yet do you know that even now, if you could bring yourself to agree with the Universities, the Bishops, and the Parliament of this realm, there is no honour which the King would be likely to deny you?

MORE   (*stonily*) I am well acquainted with His Grace's generosity.

CROMWELL   (*coldly*) Very well. (*Consults paper*). You have heard of the so-called 'Holy Maid of Kent' — who was executed for prophesying against the King?

MORE   Yes; I knew the poor woman.

CROMWELL   (*quick*) You sympathise with her?

MORE   She was ignorant and misguided; she was a bit mad I think. And she has paid for her folly. Naturally I sympathise with her.

CROMWELL   (*grunts*) You admit meeting her. You met her — and yet you did not warn His Majesty of her treason. How was that?

MORE	She spoke no treason. Our conversation was not political.
CROMWELL	My dear More, the woman was notorious! Do you expect me to believe that?
MORE	Happily there were witnesses.
CROMWELL	You wrote a letter to her?
MORE	Yes, I wrote advising her to abstain from meddling with the affairs of Princes and the State. I have a copy of this letter — also witnessed.
CROMWELL	You have been cautious.
MORE	I like to keep my affairs regular.
CROMWELL	Sir Thomas, there is a more serious charge —
MORE	Charge?
CROMWELL	For want of a better word. In the May of 1521 the King published a book, (*he permits himself a little smile*) a theological work. It was called *A Defence of the Seven Sacraments*.
MORE	Yes. (*Bitterly.*) For which he was named 'Defender of the Faith', by His Holiness the Pope.
CROMWELL	— By the Bishop of Rome. Or do you insist on 'Pope'?
MORE	No, 'Bishop of Rome' if you like. It doesn't alter his authority.
CROMWELL	Thank you, you come to the point very readily; what *is* that authority? As regards the Church in other parts of Europe; (*approaching*) for example, the Church of England. What exactly *is* the Bishop of Rome's authority?
MORE	You will find it very ably set out and defended, Master Secretary, in the King's book.
CROMWELL	The book published under the King's name would be more accurate. You wrote that book.
MORE	— I wrote no part of it.
CROMWELL	— I do not mean you actually held the pen.
MORE	— I merely answered to the best of my ability certain

questions on canon law which His Majesty put to me. As I
was bound to do.

CROMWELL — Do you deny that you *instigated* it?

MORE — It was from first to last the King's own project. This is
trivial, Master Cromwell.

CROMWELL I should not think so if I were in your place.

MORE Only two people know the truth of the matter.
Myself and the King. And, whatever he may have
said to you, he will not give evidence to support
this accusation.

CROMWELL Why not?

MORE Because evidence is given on oath, and he will not perjure
himself. If you don't know that, you don't yet know him.
(CROMWELL *looks at him viciously.*)

CROMWELL (*goes apart, formally*) Sir Thomas More, is there anything
you wish to say to me concerning the King's marriage with
Queen Anne?

MORE (*very still*) I understood I was not to be asked that again.

CROMWELL Evidently you understood wrongly. These charges —

MORE (*anger breaking through*) They are terrors for children,
Mr Secretary, not for me!

CROMWELL Then know that the King commands me to charge
you in his name with great ingratitude! And to tell
you that there never was nor never could be so
villainous a servant nor so traitorous a subject as
yourself!

MORE So I am brought here at last.

CROMWELL Brought? You brought yourself to where you stand now.

MORE Yes. Still, in another sense I was brought.

CROMWELL (*indifferent*) Oh yes. (*Official.*) You may go home now.
For the present. (*Exit* MORE.) I don't like him so well as I
did. There's a man who raises the gale and won't come out
of harbour.

*Scene change commences here, i.e., rear of stage
becoming water patterned.*

RICH	(*covert jeer*) Do you still think you can frighten him?
CROMWELL	No, he's misusing his intelligence.
RICH	What will you do now, then?
CROMWELL	(*as to an importunate child*) Oh, be quiet, Rich ... We'll do whatever's necessary. The King's a man of conscience and he wants either Sir Thomas More to bless his marriage or Sir Thomas More destroyed. Either will do.
RICH	(*shakily*) They seem odd alternatives, Secretary.
CROMWELL	Do they? That's because you're not a man of conscience. If the King destroys a man, that's proof to the King that it must have been a bad man, the kind of man a man of conscience *ought* to destroy — and of course a bad man's blessing's not worth having. So either will do.
RICH	(*subdued*) I see.
CROMWELL	Oh, there's no going back, Rich. I find we've made ourselves the keepers of this conscience. And it's ravenous.

Exit CROMWELL *and* RICH.

Enter MORE.

MORE	(*calling*) Boat! ... Boat! ... (*To himself.*) Oh, come along, it's not as bad as that ... (*Calls.*) Boat!

Enter NORFOLK. *He stops.*

(*Pleased.*) Howard! ... I can't get home. They won't bring me a boat.

NORFOLK	Do you blame them?
MORE	Is it as bad as that?
NORFOLK	It's every bit as bad as that!
MORE	(*gravely*) Then it's good of you to be seen with me.
NORFOLK	(*looking back, off*) I followed you.
MORE	(*surprised*) Were *you* followed?
NORFOLK	Probably. (*Facing him.*) So listen to what I have to say: You're behaving like a fool. You're behaving like a crank. You're not behaving like a gentleman — All right, that means nothing to you; but what about your friends?
MORE	What about them?

NORFOLK	Goddammit, you're dangerous to know!
MORE	Then don't know me.
NORFOLK	There's something further ... You must have realised by now there's a ... policy, with regards to you. (MORE *nods.*) The King is using me in it.
MORE	That's clever. That's Cromwell ... You're between the upper and the nether millstones then.
NORFOLK	I am!
MORE	Howard, you must cease to know me.
NORFOLK	I do know you! I wish I didn't but I do!
MORE	I mean as a friend.
NORFOLK	You *are* my friend!
MORE	I can't relieve you of your obedience to the King, Howard. You must relieve yourself of our friendship. No one's safe now, and you have a son.
NORFOLK	You might as well advise a man to change the colour of his hair! I'm fond of you, and there it is! You're fond of me, and there it is!
MORE	What's to be done then?
NORFOLK	(*with deep appeal*) Give in.
MORE	(*gently*) I can't give in, Howard — (*smile*) you might as well advise a man to change the colour of his eyes. I can't. Our friendship's more mutable than *that*.
NORFOLK	Oh, that's immutable is it? The one fixed point in a world of changing friendships is that Thomas More will not give in!
MORE	(*urgent to explain*) To me it *has* to be, for that's myself! Affection goes as deep in me as you I think, but only God is love right through, Howard; and *that's* my *self*.
NORFOLK	And who are you? Goddammit, man, it's disproportionate! *We're* supposed to be the arrogant ones, the proud, splenetic ones — and we've all given in! Why must you stand out? (*Quiet and quick.*) You'll break my heart.
MORE	(*moved*) We'll do it now, Howard: part, as friends, and

meet as strangers. (*He attempts to take* NORFOLK'S *hand.*)

NORFOLK (*throwing it off*) Daft, Thomas! Why d'you want to take your friendship from me? For friendship's sake! You say we'll meet as strangers and every word you've said confirms our friendship!

MORE (*takes a last affectionate look at him*) Oh, that can be remedied. (*Walks away, turns: in a tone of deliberate insult.*) Norfolk, you're a fool.

NORFOLK (*starts: then smiles and folds his arms*) *You* can't place a quarrel; you haven't the style.

MORE Hear me out. You and your class have 'given in' — as you rightly call it — because the religion of this country means nothing to you one way or the other.

NORFOLK Well, that's a foolish saying for a start; the nobility of England has always been —

MORE The nobility of England, my lord, would have snored through the Sermon on the Mount. But you'll labour like Thomas Aquinas over a rat-dog's pedigree. Now what's the name of those distorted creatures you're all breeding at the moment?

NORFOLK (*steadily, but roused towards anger by* MORE'S *tone*) An artificial quarrel's not a quarrel.

MORE Don't deceive yourself, my lord, we've had a quarrel since the day we met, our friendship was but sloth.

NORFOLK You can be cruel when you've a mind to be; but I've always known that.

MORE What's the name of those dogs? Marsh mastiffs? Bog beagles?

NORFOLK Water spaniels!

MORE And what would you do with a water spaniel that was afraid of water? You'd hang it! Well, as a spaniel is to water, so is a man to his own self. I will not give in because I oppose it — *I* do — not my pride, not my spleen, nor any other of my appetites, but *I* do — *I*! (*He goes up to him and feels him up and down like an animal.* MARGARET'S *voice is heard, well off, call-*

ing her father. MORE'S *attention is irresistibly caught by this; but he turns back determinedly to* NORFOLK.) Is there no single sinew in the midst of this that serves no appetite of Norfolk's but is, just, Norfolk? There is! Give *that* some exercise, my lord!

MARGARET   (*off, nearer*) Father?

NORFOLK   (*breathing hard*) Thomas ...

MORE   Because as you stand, you'll go before your Maker in a very ill condition!

Enter MARGARET, *below; she stops, amazed at them.*

NORFOLK   Now steady, Thomas ...

MORE   And he'll have to think that somewhere back along your pedigree — a bitch got over the wall!

NORFOLK *lashes out at him; he ducks and winces. Exit* NORFOLK.

MARGARET   Father! (*As he straightens up.*) Father, what was that?

MORE   That was Norfolk. (*Looks after him wistfully.*)

Enter ROPER.

ROPER   (*excited, almost gleeful*): Do you know, sir? Have you heard? (MORE *still looking off, unanswering. To* MARGARET.) Have you told him?

MARGARET   (*gently*) We've been looking for you, Father.

MORE *the same.*

ROPER   There's to be a new Act through Parliament, sir!

MORE   (*half-turning, half attending*) Act?

ROPER   Yes, sir — about the Marriage!

MORE   (*indifferent*) Oh. (*Turning back again.*)

ROPER *and* MARGARET *look at one another.*

MARGARET   (*puts hand on his arm*) Father, by this Act, they're going to administer an oath.

MORE   (*instantaneous attention*) An oath! (*Looks from one to other.*) On what compulsion?

ROPER   It's expected to be treason!

MORE   (*very still*) What is the oath?

ROPER   (*puzzled*) It's about the Marriage, sir.

MORE   But what is the wording?

ROPER   We don't need to know the (*contemptuous*) wording — we know what it will mean!

MORE   It will mean what the words say! An oath is *made* of words! It may be possible to take it. Or avoid it. Have we a copy of the Bill? (*To* MARGARET.)

MARGARET There's one coming out from the City.

MORE   Then let's get home and look at it. Oh, I've no boat. (*He looks off again after* NORFOLK.)

MARGARET (*gently*) What happened, Father?

MORE   I spoke, slightingly, of water spaniels. Let's get home. (*He turns and sees* ROPER *excited and truculent.*) Now listen, Will. And, Meg, you know I know you well, you listen too. God made the *angels* to show him splendour — as he made animals for innocence and plants for their simplicity. But Man he made to serve him wittily, in the tangle of his mind! If he suffers us to fall to such a case that there is no escaping, then we may stand to our tackle as best we can, and yes, Will, then we may clamour like champions … if we have the spittle for it. And no doubt it delights God to see splendour where he only looked for complexity. But it's God's part, not our own, to bring ourselves to that extremity! Our natural business lies in escaping — so let's get home and study this Bill.

Exit MORE, ROPER *and* MARGARET.

Enter COMMON MAN, *dragging basket. The rear of the stage remains water-lit in moonlight. Iron grills now descend to cover all the apertures. Also, a rack, which remains suspended, and a cage which is lowered to the floor. While this takes place the* COMMON MAN *arranges three chairs behind a table. Then he turns and watches the completion of the transformation.*

COMMON   (*aggrieved*) *Now* look! … I don't suppose anyone enjoyed
MAN   it any more than he did. Well, not much more. (*Takes from basket and dons coat and hat.*) Jailer! (*Shrugs.*)

It's a job. The pay scale being what it is they have to take a rather common type of man into the prison service. But it's a job like any other job. Bit nearer the knuckle than most perhaps.

Enter right, CROMWELL, NORFOLK, CRANMER, *who sit, and* RICH, *who stands behind them. Enter left*, MORE, *who enters the cage and lies down.*

They'd let him out if they could but for various reasons they can't. (*Twirling keys.*) I'd let him out if I could but I can't. Not without taking up residence in there myself. And he's in there already, so what'd be the point? You know the old adage? 'Better a live rat than a dead lion,' and that's about it.

An envelope descends swiftly before him. He opens it and reads: 'With reference to the old adage: Thomas Cromwell was found guilty of High Treason and executed on 28 July 1540. Norfolk was found guilty of High Treason and should have been executed on 27 January 1547 but on the night of 26 January, the King died of syphilis and wasn't able to sign the warrant. Thomas Cranmer.' (*Jerking thumb.*) That's the other one — 'was burned alive on 21 March 1556.' (*He is about to conclude but sees a postscript.*) Oh. 'Richard Rich became a Knight and Solicitor-General, a Baron and Lord Chancellor, and died in his bed.' So did I. And so, I hope (*pushing off basket*) will all of you.

He goes to MORE *and rouses him. Heavy bell strikes one.*

MORE   (*rousing*) What, again?

JAILER   Sorry, sir.

MORE   (*flops back*) What time is it?

JAILER   Just struck one, sir.

MORE   Oh, this is iniquitous!

JAILER   (*anxious*) Sir.

MORE   (*sitting up*) All right. (*Putting on slippers.*) Who's there?

JAILER   The Secretary, the Duke, and the Archbishop.

MORE   I'm flattered. (*Stands. Claps hand to hip.*)
Ooh! (*Preceded by* JAILER *limps across
stage right: he has aged and is pale, but*

his manner though wary, is relaxed: while that of the Commission is bored, tense, and jumpy.)

NORFOLK (*looks at him*) A chair for the prisoner. (*While* JAILER *brings a chair and* MORE *sits in it*, NORFOLK *rattles off*): This is the Seventh Commission to enquire into the case of Sir Thomas More, appointed by His Majesty's Council. Have you anything to say?

MORE No. (*To* JAILER.) Thank you.

NORFOLK (*sitting back*) Mr Secretary.

CROMWELL Sir Thomas — (*breaks off*) — do the witnesses attend?

RICH Mr Secretary.

JAILER Sir.

CROMWELL (*to* JAILER) Nearer! (*He advances a bit.*) Come where you can hear! (JAILER *takes up stance by* RICH. *To* MORE.) Sir Thomas, you have seen this document before?

MORE Many times.

CROMWELL It is the Act of Succession. These are the names of those who have sworn to it.

MORE I have, as you say, seen it before.

CROMWELL Will you swear to it?

MORE No.

NORFOLK Thomas, we must know plainly —

CROMWELL (*throws down document*) Your Grace, *please!*

NORFOLK Master Cromwell! (*They regard one another in hatred.*)

CROMWELL I beg Your Grace's pardon. (*Sighing, rests head in hands.*)

NORFOLK Thomas, we must know plainly whether you recognise the offspring of Queen Anne as heirs to His Majesty.

MORE The King in Parliament tells me that they are. Of course I recognise them.

NORFOLK Will you swear that you do?

MORE Yes.

NORFOLK   Then why won't you swear to the Act?

CROMWELL   (*impatient*) Because there is more than that *in*
the Act.

NORFOLK   Is that it?

MORE   (*after a pause*) Yes.

NORFOLK   Then we must find out what it is in the Act that he objects
to!

CROMWELL   Brilliant. (NORFOLK *rounds on him.*)

CRANMER   (*hastily*) Your Grace — May I try?

NORFOLK   Certainly. I've no pretension to be an expert, in Police
work.

During next speech CROMWELL *straightens up and folds
arms resignedly.*

CRANMER   (*clears throat fussily*) Sir Thomas, it states in the preamble
that the King's former marriage, to the Lady
Catherine, was unlawful, she being previously his
brother's wife and the — er — 'Pope' having no authority
to sanction it. (*Gently.*) Is that what you deny?
(*No reply.*) Is that what you dispute? (*No reply.*)
Is that what you are not sure of? (*No reply.*)

NORFOLK   Thomas, you insult the King and His Council in the person
of the Lord Archbishop!

MORE   I insult no one. I will not take the oath. I will not tell you
why I will not.

NORFOLK   Then your reasons must be treasonable!

MORE   Not 'must be'; may be.

NORFOLK   It's a fair assumption!

MORE   The law requires more than an assumption;
the law requires a fact. (CROMWELL *looks at him
and away again.*)

CRANMER   I cannot judge your legal standing in the case; but until I
know the *ground* of your objections, I can only guess your
spiritual standing too.

MORE   (*is for a second furiously affronted; then humour
overtakes him*) If you're willing to guess at that,
Your Grace, it should be a small matter to guess my
objections.

CROMWELL	(*quickly*) You do have objections to the Act?
NORFOLK	(*happily*) Well, we know *that*, Cromwell!
MORE	You don't, my lord. You may *suppose* I have objections. All you *know* is that I will not swear to it. From sheer delight to give you trouble it might be.
NORFOLK	Is it material why you won't?
MORE	It's most material. For refusing to swear my goods are forfeit and I am condemned to life imprisonment. You cannot lawfully harm me further. But if you were right in supposing I had reasons for refusing and right again in supposing my reasons to be treasonable, the law would let you cut my head off.
NORFOLK	(*he has followed with some difficulty*) Oh yes.
CROMWELL	(*admiring murmur*) Oh, well done, Sir Thomas. I've been trying to make that clear to His Grace for some time.
NORFOLK	(*hardly responds to the insult; his face is gloomy and disgusted*) Oh, confound all this ... (*With real dignity.*) I'm not a scholar, as Master Cromwell never tires of pointing out, and frankly I don't know whether the marriage was lawful or not. But damn it, Thomas, look at those names ... You know those men! Can't you do what I did, and come with us, for fellowship?
MORE	(*moved*) And when we stand before God, and you are sent to Paradise for doing according to your conscience, and I am damned for not doing according to mine, will you come with me, for fellowship?
CRANMER	So those of us whose names are there are damned, Sir Thomas?
MORE	I don't know, Your Grace. I have no window to look into another man's conscience. I condemn no one.
CRANMER	Then the matter is capable of question?
MORE	Certainly.
CRANMER	But that you owe obedience to your King is not

capable of question. So weigh a doubt against a certainty —
and sign.

MORE   Some men think the Earth is round, others think it
flat; it is a matter capable of question. But if it is flat,
will the King's command make it round? And if it is
round, will the King's command flatten it? No, I will
not sign.

CROMWELL   (*leaping up, with ceremonial indignation*) Then you have
more regard to your own doubt than you have to his
command!

MORE   For myself, I have no doubt.

CROMWELL   No doubt of what?

MORE   No doubt of my grounds for refusing this oath. Grounds I
will tell to the King alone, and which you, Mr Secretary,
will not trick out of me.

NORFOLK   Thomas —

MORE   Oh, gentlemen, can't I go to bed?

CROMWELL   You don't seem to appreciate the seriousness of your
position.

MORE   I defy anyone to live in that cell for a year and not
appreciate the seriousness of his position.

CROMWELL   Yet the State has harsher punishments.

MORE   You threaten like a dockside bully.

CROMWELL   How should I threaten?

MORE   Like a Minister of State, with justice!

CROMWELL   Oh, justice is what you're threatened with.

MORE   Then I'm not threatened.

NORFOLK   Master Secretary, I think the prisoner may retire as he
requests. Unless you, my lord — ?

CRANMER   (*pettish*) No, I see no purpose in prolonging the
interview.

NORFOLK   Then good night, Thomas.

MORE   (*hesitates*) Might I have one or two more books?

CROMWELL   You have books?

MORE   Yes.

CROMWELL   I didn't know; you shouldn't have.

MORE	(*turns to go: pauses. Desperately*) May I see my family?
CROMWELL	No! (MORE *returns to cell.*) Jailer!
JAILER	Sir!
CROMWELL	Have you ever heard the prisoner speak of the King's divorce, or the King's Supremacy of the Church, or the King's marriage?
JAILER	No, sir, not a word.
CROMWELL	If he does, you will of course report it to the Lieutenant.
JAILER	Of course, sir.
CROMWELL	You will swear an oath to that effect.
JAILER	(*cheerfully*) Certainly, sir!
CROMWELL	Archbishop?
CRANMER	(*laying cross of vestment on table*) Place your left hand on this and raise your right hand — take your hat off — Now say after me: I swear by my immortal soul — (JAILER *overlapping, repeats the oath with him*) that I will report truly anything said by Sir Thomas More against the King, the Council or the State of the Realm. So help me God. Amen.
JAILER	(*overlapping*) So help me God. Amen.
CROMWELL	And there's fifty guineas in it if you do.
JAILER	(*looks at him gravely*) Yes, sir. (*And goes.*)
CRANMER	(*hastily*) That's not to tempt you into perjury, my man!
JAILER	No sir! (*At exit pauses; to audience.*) Fifty guineas isn't tempting; fifty guineas is alarming. If he'd left it at swearing … But fifty — That's serious money. If it's worth that much now it's worth my neck presently. (*Decision.*) I want no part of it. They can sort it out between them. I feel my deafness coming on.

Exit JAILER. *The Commission rises.*

CROMWELL	Rich!
RICH	Secretary?
CROMWELL	Tomorrow morning, remove the prisoner's books.

NORFOLK	Is that necessary?
CROMWELL	(*suppressed exasperation*) Norfolk. With regards this case, the King is becoming impatient.
NORFOLK	Aye, with you.
CROMWELL	With all of us. (*He walks over to the rack*). You know the King's impatience, how commodious it is!

NORFOLK *and* CRANMER *exit.* CROMWELL *is brooding over the instrument of torture.*

RICH	Secretary!
CROMWELL	(*abstracted*) Yes ...?
RICH	Sir Redvers Llewellyn has retired.
CROMWELL	(*not listening*) Mm ...?
RICH	(*goes to other end of rack and faces him. Some indignation*) The Attorney-General for Wales. His post is vacant. You said I might approach you.
CROMWELL	(*contemptuous impatience*) Oh, not *now* ... (*Broods.*) He must submit, the alternatives are bad. While More's alive the King's conscience breaks into fresh stinking flowers every time he gets from bed. And if I bring about More's death — I plant my own, I think. There's no other good solution! He must submit! (*He whirls the windlass of the rack, producing a startling clatter from the ratchet. They look at each other. He turns it again slowly, shakes his head and lets go.*) No; the King will not permit it. (*Walks away.*) We have to find some gentler way.

The scene change commences as he says this and exit RICH *and* CROMWELL. *From night it becomes morning, cold grey light from off the grey water. And enter* JAILER *and* MARGARET.

JAILER	Wake up, Sir Thomas! Your family's here!
MORE	(*starting up. A great cry*) Margaret! What's this? You can visit me? (*Thrusts arms through cage.*) Meg. Meg. (*She goes to him. Then horrified.*) For God's sake, Meg, they've not put *you* in here?
JAILER	(*reassuring*) No-o-o, sir. Just a visit; a short one.
MORE	(*excited*) Jailer, jailer, let me out of this.

JAILER   (*stolid*) Yes, sir. I'm allowed to let you out.

MORE   Thank you. (*Goes to door of cage, gabbling while* JAILER *unlocks it.*) Thank you, thank you. (*Comes out. He and she regard each other; then she drops into a curtsey.*)

MARGARET   Good morning, Father.

MORE   (*ecstatic, wraps her to him*) Oh, good morning — Good morning. (*Enter* ALICE, *supported by* WILL. *She, like* MORE, *has aged and is poorly dressed.*) Good morning, Alice. Good morning, Will.

     ROPER *is staring at the rack in horror.* ALICE *approaches* MORE *and peers at him technically.*

ALICE   (*almost accusatory*) Husband, how do you do?

MORE   (*smiling over* MARGARET) As well as need be, Alice. Very happy now. Will?

ROPER   This is an awful place!

MORE   Except it's keeping me from you, my dears, it's not so bad. Remarkably like any other place.

ALICE   (*looks up critically*) It drips!

MORE   Yes, Too near the river. (ALICE *goes apart and sits, her face bitter.*)

MARGARET   (*disengages from him, takes basket from her mother*) We've brought you some things. (*Shows him. There is constraint between them.*) Some cheese …

MORE   Cheese.

MARGARET   And a custard …

MORE   A custard!

MARGARET   And, these other things … (*She doesn't look at him.*)

ROPER   And a bottle of wine. (*Offering it.*)

MORE   Oh. (*Mischievous.*) Is it good, son Roper?

ROPER   I don't know, sir.

MORE   (*looks at them, puzzled*) Well.

ROPER   Sir, come out! Swear to the Act! Take the oath and come out!

MORE   Is this why they let you come?

ROPER	Yes … Meg's under oath to persuade you.
MORE	(*coldly*) That was silly, Meg. How did you come to do that?
MARGARET	I wanted to!
MORE	You want me to swear to the Act of Succession?
MARGARET	'God more regards the thoughts of the heart than the words of the mouth' or so you've always told me.
MORE	Yes.
MARGARET	Then say the words of the oath and in your heart think otherwise.
MORE	What is an oath then but words we say to God?
MARGARET	That's very neat.
MORE	Do you mean it isn't true?
MARGARET	No, it's true.
MORE	Then it's a poor argument to call it 'neat', Meg. When a man takes an oath, Meg, he's holding his own self in his own hands. Like water (*cups hands*) and if he opens his fingers *then* — he needn't hope to find himself again. Some men aren't capable of this, but I'd be loathe to think your father one of them.
MARGARET	So should I …
MORE	Then —
MARGARET	There's something else I've been thinking.
MORE	Oh, Meg!
MARGARET	In any state that was half good, you would be raised up high, not here, for what you've done already.
MORE	All right.
MARGARET	It's not your fault the State's three-quarters bad.
MORE	No.
MARGARET	Then if you elect to suffer for it, you elect yourself a hero.
MORE	That's very neat. But look now … if we lived in a State where virtue was profitable, common sense would make us good, and greed would make us saintly. And we'd live like animals or angels in the happy land that *needs* no

heroes. But since in fact we see that avarice, anger, envy, pride, sloth, lust and stupidity commonly profit far beyond humility, chastity, fortitude, justice and thought, and have to choose, to be human at all ... why then perhaps we *must* stand fast a little — even at the risk of being heroes.

MARGARET (*emotional*) But in reason! Haven't you done as much as God can reasonably *want*?

MORE Well ... finally ... it isn't a matter of reason; finally it's a matter of love.

ALICE (*hostile*) You're content then, to be shut up here with mice and rats when you might be home with us?

MORE (*flinching*) Content? If they'd open a crack that wide (*between finger and thumb*) I'd be through it. (*To* MARGARET.) Well, has Eve run out of apples?

MARGARET I've not yet told you what the house is like, without you.

MORE Don't, Meg.

MARGARET What we do in the evenings, now that you're not there.

MORE Meg, have done!

MARGARET We sit in the dark because we've no candles. And we've no talk because we're wondering what they're doing to you here.

MORE The King's more merciful than you. He doesn't use the rack.

Enter JAILER

JAILER Two minutes to go, sir. I thought you'd like to know.

MORE Two minutes!

JAILER Till seven o'clock, sir. Sorry. Two minutes.

Exit JAILER.

MORE Jailer — ! (*Seizes* ROPER *by the arm.*) Will — go to him, talk to him, keep him occupied — (*Propelling him after* JAILER.)

ROPER How, sir?

MORE Anyhow! — Have you got any money?

ROPER   (*eager*) Yes!

MORE   No, don't try and bribe him! Let him play for it; he's got a pair of dice. And talk to him, you understand! And take this (*the wine*) — and mind you share it — do it properly, Will! (ROPER *nods vigorously and exits.*) Now listen, you must leave the country. All of you must leave the country.

MARGARET   And leave you here?

MORE   It makes no difference, Meg; they won't let you see me again. (*Breathlessly, a prepared speech under pressure.*) You must all go on the same day, but not on the same boat; different boats from different ports —

MARGARET   After the trial, then.

MORE   There'll be no trial, they have no case. Do this for me I beseech you?

MARGARET   Yes.

MORE   Alice? (*She turns her back.*) Alice, I command it!

ALICE   (*harshly*) Right!

MORE   (*looks into basket*) Oh, this is splendid; I know who packed this.

ALICE   (*harshly*) I packed it.

MORE   Yes. (*Eats a morsel.*) You still make superlative custard, Alice.

ALICE   Do I?

MORE   That's a nice dress you have on.

ALICE   It's my cooking dress.

MORE   It's very nice anyway. Nice colour.

ALICE   (*turns. Quietly*) By God, you think very little of me. (*Mounting bitterness.*) I know I'm a fool. But I'm no such fool as at this time to be lamenting for my dresses! Or to relish complimenting on my custard!

MORE   (*regarding her with frozen attention. He nods once or twice*) I am well rebuked. (*Holds out his hands.*) Al — !

ALICE   No! (*She remains where she is, glaring at him.*)

MORE   (*he is in great fear of her*) I am faint when I think of the worst that they may do to me. But worse than that would be to go, with you not understanding why I go.

ALICE I don't!

MORE (*just hanging on to his self-possession*) Alice, if you can tell me that you understand, I think I can make a good death, if I have to.

ALICE Your death's no 'good' to me!

MORE Alice, you must tell me that you understand!

ALICE I don't! (*She throws it straight at his head.*) I don't believe this had to happen.

MORE (*his face is drawn*) If you say that, Alice, I don't see how I'm to face it.

ALICE It's the truth!

MORE (*gasping*) You're an honest woman.

ALICE Much good may it do me! I'll tell you what I'm afraid of; that when you've gone, I shall hate you for it.

MORE (*turns from her: his face working*) Well, you mustn't, Alice, that's all. (*Swiftly she crosses the stage to him; he turns and they clasp each other fiercely*). You mustn't, you —

ALICE (*covers his mouth with her hand*) S-s-sh … As for understanding, I understand you're the best man that I ever met or am likely to; and if you go — well God knows why I suppose — though as God's my witness God's kept deadly quiet about it! And if anyone wants my opinion of the King and his Council they've only to ask for it!

MORE Why, it's a lion I married! A lion! A lion! (*He breaks away from her his face shining.*) Get them to take half this to Bishop Fisher — they've got him in the upper gallery —

ALICE It's for you, not Bishop Fisher!

MORE Now do as I ask — (*Breaks off a piece of the custard and eats it.*) Oh, it's good, it's very, very good. (*He puts his face in his hands;* ALICE *and* MARGARET *comfort him;* ROPER *and* JAILER *erupt on to the stage above, wrangling fiercely.*)

JAILER It's no good, sir! I know what you're up to! And it can't be done!

ROPER Another minute, man!

JAILER	(*to* MORE *descending*) Sorry, sir, time's up!
ROPER	(*gripping his shoulder from behind*) For pity's sake — !
JAILER	(*shaking him off*) Now don't do that, sir! Sir Thomas, the ladies will have to go now!
MORE	You said seven o'clock!
JAILER	It's seven now. You must understand my position, sir.
MORE	But one more minute!
MARGARET	Only a little while — give us a little while!
JAILER	(*reproving*) Now, Miss, you don't want to get me into trouble.
ALICE	Do as you're told. Be off at once!

The first stroke of seven is heard on a heavy, deliberate bell, which continues, reducing what follows to a babble.

JAILER	(*taking* MARGARET *firmly by the upper arm*) Now come along, Miss; you'll get your father into trouble as well as me. (ROPER *descends and grabs him.*) Are you obstructing me, sir? (MARGARET *embraces* MORE, *and dashes up the stairs and exits, followed by* ROPER. *Taking* ALICE *gingerly by the arm.*) Now, my lady, no trouble!
ALICE	(*throwing him off as she rises*) *Don't* put your muddy hand on me!
JAILER	Am I to call the guard then? Then come on!

ALICE, *facing him, puts foot on bottom stair and so retreats before him, backwards.*

MORE	For God's sake, man, we're saying good-bye!
JAILER	You don't know what you're asking, sir. You don't know how you're watched.
ALICE	Filthy, stinking, gutter-bred turnkey!
JAILER	Call me what you like, ma'am; you've got to go.
ALICE	I'll see you suffer for this!
JAILER	You're doing your husband no good!
MORE	Alice, good-bye, my love!

On this, the last stroke of the seven sounds. ALICE *raises her hand, turns, and with considerable dignity, exits.* JAILER *stops at head of stairs and addresses* MORE, *who, still crouching, turns from him, facing audience.*

JAILER   (*reasonably*) You understand my position, sir, there's nothing I can do; I'm a plain simple man and just want to keep out of trouble.

MORE   (*cries out passionately*) Oh, Sweet Jesus! These plain, simple, men!

Immediately: (1)   *Music, portentous and heraldic.*
                   (2)   *Bars, rack and cage flown swiftly upwards.*
                   (3)   *Lighting change from cold grey to warm yellow, re-creating a warm interior.*
                   (4)   *Several narrow panels, scarlet and bearing the monogram 'HR VIII' in gold are lowered. Also an enormous Royal Coat of-Arms which hangs above the table stage right.*
                   (5)   *The* JAILER, *doffing costume comes down the stairs and:*

(A)   *Places a chair for the Accused, helps* MORE *to it, and gives him a scroll which he studies.*

(B)   *Fetches from the wings his prop basket, and produces: (I) A large hour-glass and papers which he places on table, stage right. (II) Twelve folding stools which he arranges in two rows of six each. While he is still doing this, and just before the panels and Coat-of-Arms have finished their descent, enter* CROMWELL. *He ringingly addresses the audience (while the* COMMON MAN *is still bustling about his chores) as soon as the music ends, which it does at this point, on a fanfare.*

CROMWELL   (*indicating descending props*):

            What Englishman can behold without Awe
            The Canvas and the Rigging of the Law!

(*Brief fanfare.*)

            Forbidden here the galley-master's whip —
            Hearts of Oak, in the Law's Great Ship!

(*Brief fanfare.*)

(*To* COMMON MAN *who is tiptoeing discreetly off stage.*)
Where are you going?

COMMON MAN I've finished here, sir.

Above the two rows of stools the COMMON MAN *has suspended from two wires, supported by two pairs of sticks, two rows of hats for the presumed occupants. Seven are plain grey hats, four are those worn by the* STEWARD, BOATMAN, INNKEEPER *and* JAILER. *And the last is another of the plain grey ones. The basket remains on stage, clearly visible.*

CROMWELL You're the Foreman of the Jury.

COMMAN MAN Oh no, sir.

CROMWELL You are John Dauncey. A general dealer?

COMMON MAN (*gloomy*) Yes, sir?

CROMWELL (*resuming his rhetorical stance*) Foreman of the Jury. Does the cap fit?

COMMON MAN *puts on the grey hat. It fits.*

COMMON MAN Yes, sir.

CROMWELL (*resuming rhetorical stance*)

So, now we'll apply the good, plain sailor's art,
And fix these quicksands on the Law's plain chart!

Renewed, more prolonged fanfare, during which enter CRANMER *and* NORFOLK, *who stand behind the table stage right. On their entry* MORE *and* FOREMAN *rise. So soon as fanfare is finished* NORFOLK *speaks.*

NORFOLK (*takes refuge behind a rigorously official manner*) Sir Thomas More, you are called before us here at the Hall of Westminster to answer charge of High Treason. Nevertheless, and though you have heinously offended the King's Majesty, we hope if you will even now forthink and repent of your obstinate opinions, you may still taste his gracious pardon.

MORE My lords, I thank you. Howbeit I make my petition to Almighty God that he will keep me in this, my honest mind to the last hour that I shall live ... As for the matters you may charge me with, I fear, from my present weakness, that

    neither my wit nor my memory will serve to make
    sufficient answers … I should be glad to sit down.

NORFOLK Be seated. Master Secretary Cromwell, have you the charge?

CROMWELL I have, my lord.

NORFOLK Then read the charge.

CROMWELL (*approaching* MORE, *behind him, with papers; informally*)
    It is the same charge, Sir Thomas, that was brought against
    Bishop Fisher … (*As one who catches himself up
    punctiliously.*) The *late* Bishop Fisher, I should have said.

MORE (*tonelessly*) 'Late'?

CROMWELL Bishop Fisher was executed this morning.

    MORE'S *face expresses violent shock, then grief; he turns his
    head away from* CROMWELL *who is observing him clinically.*

NORFOLK Master Secretary, read the charge!

CROMWELL (*formal*) That you did conspire traitorously and
    maliciously to deny and deprive our liege lord Henry
    of his undoubted certain title, Supreme Head of the
    Church in England.

MORE (*surprise, shock, and indignation*) But I have never denied
    this title!

CROMWELL You refused the oath tendered to you at the Tower and
    elsewhere —

MORE (*the same*) Silence is not denial. And for my silence I am
    punished with imprisonment. Why have I been called again
    (*At this point he is sensing that the trial has been in some
    way rigged.*)

NORFOLK On a charge of High Treason, Sir Thomas.

CROMWELL For which the punishment is *not* imprisonment.

MORE Death … comes for us all, my lords. Yes, even for Kings
    he comes, to whom amidst all their Royalty and
    brute strength he will neither kneel nor make
    them any reverence nor pleasantly desire them to
    come forth, but roughly grasp them by the very breast
    and rattle them until they be stark dead! So
    causing their bodies to be buried in a pit and send-

ing *them* to a judgement ... whereof at their death their success is uncertain.

CROMWELL Treason enough here!

NORFOLK The death of Kings is not in question, Sir Thomas.

MORE Nor mine, I trust, until I'm proven guilty.

NORFOLK (*leaning forward urgently*) Your life lies in your own hand, Thomas, as it always has.

MORE (*absorbs this*) For our own deaths, my lord, yours and mine, dare we for shame desire to enter the Kingdom with ease, when Our Lord Himself entered with so much pain?

And now he faces CROMWELL *his eyes sparkling with suspicion.*

CROMWELL Now, Sir Thomas, you stand upon your silence.

MORE I do.

CROMWELL But, Gentlemen of the Jury, there are many kinds of silence. Consider first the silence of a man when he is dead. Let us say we go into the room where he is lying; and let us say it is in the dead of night — there's nothing like darkness for sharpening the ear; and we listen. What do we hear? Silence. What does it betoken, this silence? Nothing. This is silence, pure and simple. But consider another case. Suppose I were to draw a dagger from my sleeve and make to kill the prisoner with it, and suppose their lordships there, instead of crying out for me to stop or crying out for help to stop me, maintained their silence. That *would* betoken! It would betoken a willingness that I should do it, and under the law they would be guilty with me. So silence can, according to circumstances, speak. Consider now, the circumstances of the prisoner's silence. The oath was put to good and faithful subjects up and down the country and they had declared His Grace's Title to be just and good. And when it came to the prisoner he refused. He calls this silence. Yet is there a man in this court, is there a man in this country, who does not *know* Sir Thomas More's opinion of this title? Of course not! But how can that be? Because this silence betokened — nay this silence *was* — not silence at all, but most eloquent denial.

MORE (*with some of his academic's impatience for a shoddy line of reasoning*) Not so, Mr Secretary, the maxim is 'qui tacet consentire'. (*Turns to* COMMON MAN.) The maxim of the law is: (*very carefully*) 'Silence Gives Consent'. If therefore, you wish to construe what my silence 'betokened', you must construe that I consented, not that I denied.

CROMWELL Is that what the world in fact construes from it? Do you pretend that is what you *wish* the world to construe from it?

MORE The world must construe according to its wits. This Court must construe according to the law.

CROMWELL I put it to the Court that the prisoner is preventing the law — making smoky what should be a clear light to discover to the Court his own wrongdoing! (CROMWELL'S *official indignation is slipping into genuine anger and* MORE *responds.*)

MORE The law is not a 'light' for you or any man to see by; the law is not an instrument of any kind. (*To the* FOREMAN.) The law is a causeway upon which so long as he keeps to it a citizen may walk safely. (*Earnestly addressing him.*) In matters of conscience —

CROMWELL (*bitterly smiling*) The conscience, the conscience …

MORE (*turning*) The word is not familiar to you?

CROMWELL By God, too familiar! I am very used to hear it in the mouths of criminals!

MORE I am used to hear bad men misuse the name of God, yet God exists. (*Turning back.*) In matters of conscience, the loyal subject is more bounden to be loyal *to* his conscience than to any other thing.

CROMWELL (*breathing hard: straight at* MORE) And so provide a noble motive for his frivolous self-conceit!

MORE (*earnestly*) It is not so, Master Cromwell — very and pure necessity for respect of my own soul.

CROMWELL	— Your own self you mean!
MORE	Yes, a man's soul is his self!
CROMWELL	(*thrusts his face into* MORE'S. *They hate each other and each other's standpoint*) A miserable thing, whatever you call it, that lives like a bat in a Sunday School! A shrill incessant pedagogue about its own salvation — but nothing to say of your place in the State! Under the King! In a great native country!
MORE	(*not untouched*) Can I help my King by giving him lies when he asks for truth? Will you help England by populating her with liars?
CROMWELL	(*backs away. His face stiff with malevolence*) My lords, I wish to call (*raises voice*) Sir Richard Rich!

Enter RICH. *He is now splendidly official, in dress and bearing; even* NORFOLK *is a bit impressed.*

Sir Richard (*indicating* CRANMER).

CRANMER	(*proffering Bible*) I do solemnly swear …
RICH	I do solemnly swear that the evidence I shall give before the Court shall be the truth, the whole truth, and nothing but the truth.
CRANMER	(*discreetly*) So help me God, Sir Richard.
RICH	So help me God.
NORFOLK	Take your stand there, Sir Richard.
CROMWELL	Now, Rich, on 12 March, you were at the Tower?
RICH	I was.
CROMWELL	With what purpose?
RICH	I was sent to carry away the prisoner's books.
CROMWELL	Did you talk with the prisoner?
RICH	Yes.
CROMWELL	Did you talk about the King's Supremacy of the Church?
RICH	Yes.
CROMWELL	What did you say?
RICH	I said to him: 'Supposing there was an Act of Parliament

to say that I, Richard Rich, were to be King, would not you, Master More, take me for King? 'That I would,' he said, 'for then you would be King.'

CROMWELL   Yes?

RICH   Then he said —

NORFOLK   (*sharply*) The prisoner?

RICH   Yes, my lord. 'But I will put you a higher case,' he said. 'How if there were an Act of Parliament to say that God should not be God?'

MORE   This is true; and then you said —

NORFOLK   Silence! Continue.

RICH   I said 'Ah, but I will put you a middle case. Parliament has made our King Head of the Church. Why will you not accept him?'

NORFOLK   (*strung up*) Well?

RICH   Then he said Parliament had no power to do it.

NORFOLK   Repeat the prisoner's words!

RICH   He said 'Parliament has not the competence.' Or words to that effect.

CROMWELL   He denied the title?

RICH   He did.

All look to MORE *but he looks to* RICH.

MORE   In good faith, Rich, I am sorrier for your perjury than my peril.

NORFOLK   Do you deny this?

MORE   Yes! My lords, if I were a man who heeded not the taking of an oath, you know well I need not to be here. Now I will take an oath! If what Master Rich has said is true, then I pray I may never see God in the face! Which I would not say were it otherwise for anything on earth.

CROMWELL   (*to* FOREMAN, *calmly, technical*) That is not evidence.

MORE   Is it probable — is it probable — that after so long a silence, on this, the very point so urgently sought of me, I should open my mind to such a man as that?

CROMWELL   (*to* RICH) Do you wish to modify your testimony?

RICH   No, Secretary.

MORE   There were two other men! Southwell and Palmer!

CROMWELL   Unhappily, Sir Richard Southwell and Master Palmer are both in Ireland on the King's business. (MORE *gestures helplessly.*) It has no bearing. I have their deposition here in which the Court will see they state that being busy with the prisoner's books they did not hear what was said. (*Hands deposition to* FOREMAN *who examines it with much seriousness.*)

MORE   If I had really said this is it not obvious he would instantly have called these men to witness?

CROMWELL   Sir Richard, have you anything to add?

RICH   Nothing, Mr Secretary.

NORFOLK   Sir Thomas?

MORE   (*looking at* FOREMAN) To what purpose? I am a dead man. (*To* CROMWELL.) You have your desire of me. What you have hunted me for is not my actions, but the thoughts of my heart. It is a long road you have opened. For first men will disclaim their hearts and presently they will have no hearts. God help the people whose Statesmen walk your road.

NORFOLK   Then the witness may withdraw.

RICH *crosses stage, watched by* MORE.

MORE   I *have* one question to ask the witness. (RICH *stops.*) That's a chain of office you are wearing. (*Reluctantly* RICH *faces him.*) May I see it? (NORFOLK *motions him to approach,* MORE *examines the medallion.*) The red dragon. (*To* CROMWELL.) What's this?

CROMWELL   Sir Richard is appointed Attorney-General for Wales.

MORE   (*looking into* RICH'S *face: with pain and amusement*) For Wales? Why, Richard, it profits a man nothing to give his soul for the whole world ... But for Wales — !

Exit RICH, *stiff faced, but infrangibly dignified.*

CROMWELL   Now I must ask the Court's indulgence! I have a message
              for the prisoner from the King: (*urgent*) Sir Thomas, I am
              empowered to tell you that even now —

MORE   No no. It cannot be.

CROMWELL   The case rests! (NORFOLK *is staring at* MORE.) My lord!

NORFOLK   The Jury will retire and consider the evidence.

CROMWELL   Considering the evidence it shouldn't be necessary
              for them to retire. (*Standing over* FOREMAN.) Is it
              necessary?

              FOREMAN *shakes his head.*

NORFOLK   Then is the prisoner guilty or not guilty?

FOREMAN   Guilty, my lord!

NORFOLK   (*leaping to his feet; all rise save* MORE) Prisoner at the bar,
              you have been found guilty of High Treason. The sentence
              of the Court —

MORE   My lord!

              NORFOLK *breaks off.* MORE *has a sly smile. From this
              point to end of play his manner is of one who has
              fulfilled all his obligations and will now consult
              no interests but his own.*

              My lord, when *I* was practising the law, the manner was to
              ask the prisoner *before* pronouncing sentence, if he had
              anything to say.

NORFOLK   (*flummoxed*) Have you anything to say?

MORE   Yes. (*He rises: all others sit.*) To avoid this I have
              taken every path my winding wits would find. Now
              that the court has determined to condemn me, God
              knoweth how, I will discharge my mind … concerning
              my indictment and the King's title. The indictment is
              grounded in an Act of Parliament which is directly
              repugnant to the Law of God. The King in Parliament
              cannot bestow the Supremacy of the Church because
              it is a Spiritual Supremacy! And more to this the
              immunity of the Church is promised both in
              Magna Carta and the King's own Coronation Oath!

CROMWELL   Now we plainly see that you *are* malicious!

MORE   Not so, Mr Secretary! (*He pauses, and launches, very quietly, ruminatively, into his final stock-taking.*) I am the King's true subject, and pray for him and all the realm ... I do none harm, I say none harm, I think none harm. And if this be not enough to keep a man alive, in good faith I long not to live ... I have, since I came into prison, been several times in such a case that I thought to die within the hour, and I thank Our Lord I was never sorry for it, but rather sorry when it passed. And therefore, my poor body is at the King's pleasure. Would God my death might do him some good... (*With a great flash of scorn and anger.*) Nevertheless, it is not for the Supremacy that you have sought my blood — but because I would not bend to the marriage!

Immediately scene change commences, while NORFOLK *reads the sentence.*

NORFOLK   Prisoner at the bar, you have been found guilty on the charge of High Treason. The sentence of the Court is that you shall be taken from this Court to the Tower, thence to the place of execution, and there your head shall be stricken from your body, and may God have mercy on your soul!

The scene change is as follows:

(I)   *The trappings of justice are flown upwards.*

(II) *The lights are dimmed save for three areas: spots, left and right front, and the arch at the head of the stairs which begins to show blue sky.*

(III) *Through this arch — where the axe and the block are silhouetted against a light of steadily increasing brilliance — comes the murmuration of a large crowd, formalised almost into a chant and mounting, so that* NORFOLK *has to shout the end of his speech.*

In addition to the noise of the crowd and the flying machinery there is stage activity: FOREMAN *doffs cap, and as* COMMON MAN *removes the prisoner's chair and then goes to the spot, left.*

CRANMER *also goes to spot, left.*

MORE *goes to spot, right.*

WOMAN *enters, up right, and goes to spot, left.*

NORFOLK *remains where he is.*

When these movements are complete — they are made naturally, technically — CROMWELL *goes and stands in the light streaming down the stairs. He beckons the* COMMON MAN *who leaves spot, left, and joins him.* CROMWELL *points to the head of the stairs.* COMMON MAN *shakes his head and indicates in mime that he has no costume. He drags basket into the light and again indicates that there is no costume in it.* CROMWELL *takes a small black mask from his sleeve and offers it to him. The* COMMON MAN *puts it on, thus, in his black tights, becoming the traditional heads-man. He ascends the stairs, straddles his legs and picks up the axe, silhouetted against the bright sky. At once the crowd falls silent.*

Exit CROMWELL, *dragging basket.*

NORFOLK *joins* MORE *in spot, right.*

NORFOLK   I can come no further, Thomas. (*Proffering goblet.*) Here, drink this.

MORE   My master had easel and gall, not wine, given him to drink. Let me be going.

MARGARET   Father! (*She runs to him in the spot from right and flings herself upon him.*) Father! Father, Father, Father, Father!

MORE   Have patience, Margaret, and trouble not thyself. Death comes for us all; even at our birth (*he holds her head and looks down at it for a moment in recollection*) — even at our birth, death does but stand aside a little. It is the law of nature, and the will of God. (*He disengages from her. Dispassionately.*) You have long known the secrets of my heart.

WOMAN   Sir Thomas! (*He stops.*) Remember me, Sir Thomas? When you were Chancellor, you gave a false judgement against me. Remember that now.

MORE   Woman, you see how I am occupied. (*With sudden decision goes to her in spot, left. Crisply.*) I remember your matter well, and if I had to give sentence now I assure you I should not alter it. You have no injury; so go your ways;

and content yourself; and trouble me not! (*He walks swiftly to the stairs. Then stops, realising that* CRANMER, *carrying his Bible, has followed him. Quite kindly.*) I beseech Your Grace, go back.

Offended, CRANMER *does so. The lighting is now complete, i.e., darkness save for three areas of light, the one at head of stairs now dazzlingly brilliant. When* MORE *gets to head of stairs by the* HEADSMAN *there is a single shout from the crowd. He turns to* HEADSMAN.

Friend, be not afraid of your office. You send me to God.

CRANMER (*envious rather than waspish*) You're very sure of that, Sir Thomas.

MORE (*takes off his hat, revealing the grey disordered hair*) He will not refuse one who is so blithe to go to him. (*Kneeling.*)

Immediately, harsh roar of kettledrums and total blackout at head of stairs. While the drums roar, WOMAN *backs into* CRANMER *and exit together.* NORFOLK *assists* MARGARET *from the stage, which is now 'occupied' only by the two spots left and right front. The drums cease.*

HEADSMAN (*from the darkness*) Behold — the head — of a traitor!

Enter into spots left and right, CROMWELL *and* CHAPUYS. *They stop on seeing one another, arrested in postures of frozen hostility while the light spreads plainly over the stage, which is empty save for themselves.*

Then simultaneously they stalk forward, crossing mid-stage with heads high and averted. But as they approach their exits they pause, hesitate, and slowly turn. Thoughtfully they stroll back towards one another. CROMWELL *raises his head and essays a smile.* CHAPUYS *responds. They link arms and approach the stairs. As they go we hear that they are chuckling. There is nothing sinister or malignant in the sound; rather it is the self-mocking, self-indulgent, rather rueful laughter of men who know what the world is and how to be comfortable in it. As they go,* THE CURTAIN FALLS.

ALTERNATIVE ENDING

In the London production of this play at the Globe Theatre the play ended as follows:

Instead of the CROMWELL *and* CHAPUYS *entrance after the* HEADSMAN'S *line* 'Behold — the head — of a traitor!', *the* COMMON MAN *came to the centre stage, having taken off his mask as the executioner, and said:*

'I'm breathing … Are you breathing too? … It's nice isn't it? It isn't difficult to keep alive friends … just don't make trouble — or if you must make trouble, make the sort of trouble that's expected. Well, I don't need to tell you that. Good night. If we should bump into one another, recognise me.'

(*Exits*)

CURTAIN

QUESTIONS AND EXPLORATIONS

1 Keeping Track

The questions in this section are designed to help your reading and understanding of the play in the areas of plot, character, structure and interaction. They may be used as you read the play or afterwards, for discussion or for writing. Some are developed and expanded in the Explorations section.

Act One

Section One: Pages 1-9

1 Describe the attitude of the Common Man.

2 What do we learn about More's attitude to his position?

3 What do we learn about Richard Rich? Why does More give him the goblet?

4 What do we learn about the Duke of Norfolk?

5 Why is Cromwell disliked?

6 What do we learn about the More family's relationships?

Section Two: Pages 9-20

7 What is the Common Man's attitude to More?

8 What do we learn about Wolsey's character from his treatment of More?

9 Where has the King been?

10 Why is More wary of Wolsey?

11 Summarize the political problem the King faces: what is the solution Wolsey prefers?

12 What is More's attitude to this solution? Why?

13 Why does Cromwell appear so suddenly?

14 What is Chapuys' interest in More?

15 Why will More not allow Margaret to marry Roper?

16 What is Alice's attitude to her husband?

Section 3: Pages 20-41

17 What is the Common Man's attitude to Wolsey's fall and More's promotion?

18 How has the pressure on More increased as a result?

19 How does the Steward exploit the situation?

20 What do we learn about the character of King Henry on his arrival at the Mores' house?

21 How does Henry feel about Wolsey's failure to achieve the divorce?

22 Why can More not give his consent to the divorce?

23 And why is Henry so desperate for More's support?

24 What is More's attitude to Henry during their conversation?

25 What is the compromise Henry offers to More?

26 What is Alice afraid of for More?

27 How have Roper's ideas about the church changed?

28 What are Rich's reasons for visiting More?

29 Why does More insist on following the law and not arresting Rich?

30 What is More's opinion of Roper's principles?

Section 4: Pages 41-46

31 Why is Cromwell collecting information about More?

32 What effect does Cromwell have on Rich?

33 What does Cromwell want to know about the goblet Rich received from More? How will he use this information?

34 Why does Cromwell burn Rich?

Act Two

Section One: Pages 47-57

1 What has happened during the interval?

2 Why does More attach importance to the phrase 'so far as the law of God allows'?

3 Why does Chapuys visit More?

4 Why does More resign as Chancellor?

5 Why is More keen to make himself 'obscure'?

6 How do the different members of his family react to his actions?

7 Why does More intend to remain silent?

Section Two: Pages 57-75

8 How does Cromwell intend to secure More's support?

9 How has the atmosphere in the More household changed?

10 Why will More not take King Charles's letter from Chapuys?

11 Why will More not accept the Bishop's charity?

12 And how does his family feel about this?

13 How would More react on seeing Rich at work for Cromwell?

14 What is the result of More's interview with Cromwell?

15 What is Norfolk's advice to More?

16 Why does More provoke Norfolk?

17 Why is Parliament introducing the new Act of Succession?

Section Three: Pages 75-88

18 Why does the Common Man/Jailer tell us of Cromwell's, Cranmer's and Norfolk's fate but not More's?

19 What defence does More adopt against the Commission?

20 What reactions does this provoke from them?

21 How is More's imprisonment affecting him? How would an actor show this in performance?

22 Why is More's family allowed to visit him?

23 What arguments does Margaret use to try to persuade him?

24 And how does More resist them?

25 What is Alice's attitude to More?

26 And how does it affect him?

27 How, in performance, would the More family part?

Section Four: Pages 88-101

28 Why is More tried for treason?

29 What is Cromwell's case against More?

30 How does More make his defence?

31 How, as More senses, has the trial been 'rigged'?

32 How does More's attitude change after the verdict?

33 How would More deliver the final statement to the court?

34 How would he go to his execution?

35 What does the Common Man mean by 'It isn't difficult to keep alive'?

2 Explorations

The questions in this section are more detailed and rely on your having read the whole play. Some of the questions develop ideas from the Keeping Track section. Because they tend to be more detailed, they offer the opportunity to develop the ideas into written, oral or practical coursework assignments. Some will require a close knowledge of the play; others will require a more imaginative response.

A Characters

More

1 'Buy a man with suffering?' Explain how More's actions in the play lead to his suffering the ultimate punishment.

2 'You're too nice altogether, Thomas!' Explain the qualities and characteristics that make More the man he is in the play.

3 'The Lord Chancellor is not an ordinary subject. He bears responsibility for what is done.' Explain why More is unable to bear the responsibility of his office.

4 'What does it betoken, this silence?' Why does More take refuge in silence? Why does this policy fail?

5 'I do none harm, I say none harm, I think none harm.' Show how, in the play, More's goodness becomes his fatal flaw.

6 'Behold - the head - of a traitor!' Show how More becomes a traitor in the play.

7 Paying attention to characterization and expression, write the letters More would have sent to each of the following before his execution:
   (i)   King Henry
   (ii)   Alice and Margaret
   (iii) Richard Rich
   (iv)   Thomas Cromwell.

The More family

8 'I don't believe this had to happen.' How are Alice and Margaret affected by the events of the play? How do they react to them?

9 'We must pray, that when your head has finished turning your face is to the front again.' Explain what Roper believes in as the play develops.

10 Paying attention to characterization and expression, write the final letters that Alice, Margaret and Roper would have sent to More before his death.

Henry VIII

11 'No opposition, I say! No opposition!' Explain how the character of Henry VIII drives the actions of the characters in the play.

Norfolk

12 'You're between the upper and the nether millstones then.' Explain Norfolk's actions and involvement in the course of the play.

13 'You must relieve yourself of our friendship.' Show how the friendship between More and Norfolk is affected by the events of the play.

Cromwell

14 'When the King wants something done, I do it.' By explaining his actions, analyse the character of Cromwell in the play.

15 'It'll be up quick and down quick with Master Cromwell.' How does Cromwell affect those with whom he comes into contact?

16 Paying attention to character and expression, write the report that Cromwell would submit to the King concerning the trial of Sir Thomas More.

Richard Rich

17 'But every man has his price.' Show how Rich gains advancement during the course of the play.

The Common Man

18 'The Sixteenth Century is the Century of the Common Man.' Who does the Common Man refer to by this? What does he mean?

19 'Better a live rat than a dead lion.' Giving examples from the text, explain the Common Man's attitude to life.

General

20 Cromwell and Chapuys are described as men who know what the world is and are comfortable in it. How do the various characters in the play - Cromwell, Chapuys, Rich, Norfolk, More - survive, or otherwise, in the world of the play?

B Themes

1 'But every man has his price.' Show the part that corruption plays in the action of *A Man for All Seasons*.

2 'The Lord Chancellor is not an ordinary subject. He bears responsibility for what is done.' What do More and Cromwell each see to be their responsibility? How do they each seek to meet it?

3 'I'm not an inconvenient man, Meg, - I've got an inconvenient conscience.' What part does conscience play in determining the course of *A Man for All Seasons*?

4 'I know what's legal, not what's right. And I'll stick to what's legal.' How is the law both used and abused by the characters in the play?

5 'A man should go where he won't be tempted.' What are the temptations offered to both More and Rich in the play? How do they deal with them?

6 'What is an oath but what we say to God?' What part does honesty play in determining the events of *A Man for All Seasons*?

7 'We'll do whatever's necessary.' Show how political power works in the world of the play.

8 'The Church is already a wing of the Palace, is it not?' Show how religious feeling plays its part in the development of the events of the play.

C In performance

1 Using the stage directions from both acts of the play, draw up a set design brief. What basic setting would be required? What other furniture and props would be required to create an effective setting successfully? Present your ideas in notes, writing or as designs.

2 Select one of the major characters. What aspects of that character would you need, as an actor, to highlight for the benefit of the audience? How would you use voice, gesture and movement to achieve this?

3 Select an extract from the play. How would you direct that extract in order to make it successful for an audience? Refer to speech, gesture, movement and expression and interaction as necessary.

4 What costumes are required for a successful presentation of the play? Showing evidence of your research, draw up a costume design brief, with costume ideas, for a selected character.

5 Design and create a poster for a production of the play at your local theatre. Consider how to attract a potential audience; explain your choice and presentation of design.

D Criticism

1 'Buy a man with suffering?' Show why More's actions lead
   ultimately to his death.

2 'Thomas More, as I wrote about him, became for me a man with
   an adamantine sense of his own self' (Bolt). Explain More's actions
   in the play in the light of this statement.

3 'He is called the Common Man to indicate that which is common
   to us all' (Bolt). What qualities does Bolt give the Common Man
   that are shared by mankind generally?

4 Explain the character and the dramatic function of the Common
   Man.

5 Trace how More's actions affect his family, giving quotations from
   the text as appropriate.

6 Quoting from the text as necessary, analyse the character and
   successful rise of Richard Rich.

7 'The King's Ear.' Show how Cromwell's function as a politician
   determines his action in the play.

8 Giving quotations as appropriate, explain how Bolt uses water
   imagery to reflect the themes of the play.

9 '… if you must make trouble, make the sort of trouble that's
   expected.' Explain fully what an audience is intended to take from
   the play, quoting as appropriate.

NOTES

1	**property basket**	the container in which the Common Man keeps the various items for the play.
	House of Lords	the upper House of Parliament, composed of the aristocracy and senior Churchmen.
	Old Adam	referring to the first man created by God, who committed the original sin.
	Common Man	Common, as in both everyday and possessing qualities shared by mankind in general.
	Household Steward	chief servant, a paid position.
2	**Signor Machiavelli**	Niccolo Machiavelli, an Italian renaissance politician, who argued in his book *The Prince* that any means to an end is appropriate, if successful. This could lead, in turn, to corrupt behaviour.
3	**Master Cromwell**	referring to Thomas Cromwell, who will later appear. As will be seen, by political cunning and determination, Cromwell rose to great power.
	Cambridge	Cambridge University.
	the Cardinal	Cardinal Wolsey, also later to appear.
	The Dean of St Paul's	St Paul's Cathedral in the City of London. John Colet, the Dean, founded a school there.
4	**Court of Requests**	one of the Tudor courts of law.
5	**Duke of Norfolk**	a nobleman, a member of the King's Council.
6	**Aristotle**	A leading ancient Greek philosopher.
	God's body	Alice is swearing.
	City Wife	a merchant's, rather than a lawyer's wife.

7	**farrier**	blacksmith.
8	**The Queen's business**	the proposed royal divorce.
	Richmond	Cardinal Wolsey's palace.
	The New Inn	one of the London Inns of Court, a training ground for lawyers.
	Hounslow	an area outside London used for hunting.
10	**the Latin dispatch**	letters to and from the Pope in Rome were written in the official language of the Catholic Church: Latin.
	the Council	The King's Council existed to advise the King, but Henry appointed those he could rely on in order to ensure it provided the right advice.
11	**play in the muck**	a reference to Henry VIII's affair with Anne Boleyn.
	two Tudors	Henry VIII was the second Tudor King, following his father Henry VII who won the Crown following the Wars of the Roses (see below) but at present Henry VIII has no son and heir.
	Catherine	Catherine of Aragon, an area of Spain; the King's wife who had previously been married to Henry's older brother Arthur who had died.
	a dispensation	special permission had been granted by the Pope to allow Henry to marry his brother's widow, Catherine of Aragon.
12	**the Yorkist Wars**	the Wars of the Roses, effectively a civil war in England, ended when Henry Tudor defeated Richard III to become Henry VII.
13	**Fisher? Suffolk?**	Thomas Fisher was Bishop of Rochester. The Earl of Suffolk was Henry's brother-in-law.
14	**Chapuys**	The Spanish ambassador of Charles V of Spain, Catherine of Aragon's nephew.

15	**Dominus vobiscum . . . spiritu tuo**	God be with you . . . and your spirit.
16	**called to the Bar**	became a qualified barrister, able to work as a lawyer.
17	**advocates**	senior barristers
	heretic	someone who disbelieved in the teaching of the Catholic Church.
	Luther	Martin Luther, a German preacher who started the Reformation by attacking corruption in the Catholic Church, leading to the establishment of breakaway Protestant churches.
	excommunicate	Luther had been cut off from the Catholic church by the Pope.
19	**Chancellor**	one of the most powerful positions in the government.
	The Tower	the Tower of London, used as a prison at this time.
20	**Professor Larcomb**	an invented historian.
	pulmonary pneumonia	lung disease.
	Hampton Court	Wolsey's residence near Richmond.
21	**Deptford**	on the River Thames, the royal shipyards.
22	**Chelsea**	the area on the river where More lives, between Westminster and Richmond.
23	**Lent**	the period leading up to Easter in which Christians give up something they like in symbolic suffering.
	Dominican	a particularly strict order of monks.
25	**plainsong**	an early form of church music.
26	**a cassock**	a clergyman's gown
	Vespers	the evening service of the church.
27	**a cloth of gold**	a rich weave of silk and gold.
28	**Oxford Latin**	the University of Oxford taught its own version of the dead language of Latin.

29	**Your Grace's Book**	Henry's book, *A Defence of the Seven Sacraments*, in which he wrote against Luther's heresies and so defended the Catholic Church.
30	**Bishop of Rome**	meaning the Pope, implying a lack of respect for the Pope and, as a result, the Catholic Church.
31	**the Great Seal**	the Chancellor's badge of office.
	Leviticus and Deuteronomy	the two books of the Bible which contradict each other. Deuteronomy had allowed Henry to marry Catherine; he now uses Leviticus as a reason for divorcing her.
32	**Holy See**	the papacy and its jurisdiction.
33	**the Emperor's knife**	King Charles, King of Spain, Holy Roman Emperor and Catherine of Aragon's nephew, had occupied Rome and hence, held the Pope in his power.
35	**Lady Anne**	Anne Boleyn.
36	**Joshua's trumpet**	according to the Bible, the prophet Joshua achieved the destruction of the walls of the city of Jericho by the blowing of trumpets.
	offered a seat in the next Parliament	Parliament was non-elected.
	sophistication	deviousness, evasiveness.
39	**the golden calf**	a metaphor for anything which is falsely worshipped.
	Moloch	a cruel Old Testament heathen god.
40	**Burgundy**	a French red wine.
41	**The Loyal Subject**	the pub's name.
45	**Court of Requests**	the court where More was sitting in judgement, which dealt with people's grievances.

Act Two

page

47	**The Church of England**	the new Church, created by an Act of Parliament, of which the King, not the Pope, was the Supreme Head.
48	**Convocation**	the bishops' assembly.
	The Act of Supremacy	the act of parliament by which the king was granted the power to make laws for the church as well as the state.
	High Treason	acting against the state, punishable by death.
49	**Socrates**	a highly respected ancient Greek philosopher who died of hemlock poisoning.
	Erasmus	a great Dutch scholar and contemporary of More.
	hemlock	a poison, used to kill Socrates.
	Cheapside	a business district in London.
51	**Yorkshire and Northumberland**	northern counties in England in which Catholicism remained strong and in which resentment simmered over Henry's reforms.
53	**The Apostolic Succession**	the theory that each new Pope was a successor of the first Pope, the apostle St Peter.
54	**the Old Alliance**	of Scotland and France against England.
	Dago	an insulting reference to Chapuys.
	make goslings in the ash	draw pictures, idly in the ash from the hearth.
55	**Like David with a harp!**	According to the Bible, David danced with all his might to show his love of God.
58	**Cato**	a judge of the Roman Empire, renowned for his honesty and morality.
61	**This isn't Spain**	Cromwell refers to the torture and execution of religious prisoners in Spain.

62	**Royal Commission**	an official message from the King of Spain.
63	**King Charles**	the King of Spain, Catherine of Aragon's nephew.
64	**bracken**	a fern which the More family are reduced to using as fuel for heating and cooking.
	the money from the Bishops	More had been offered money by the Church for his writings against heretics.
66	**witty**	clever, quick-thinking, wise.
	the merest plumber	a workman, lacking in flair, is More's opinion of Cromwell.
67	**the Universities, the Bishops and the Parliament**	all of whom Henry had consulted about the wisdom of his divorce, and all of whom had agreed with him.
	Holy Maid of Kent	a nun named Anne Barton who while undergoing fits condemned the royal divorce. Although More tried to ensure her a fair trial, she was eventually executed.
69	**canon law**	church law.
71	**upper and nether millstones**	More sympathizes with Norfolk, he says he is caught like crushed corn between the grindstones of a mill, metaphorically speaking.
	you have a son	Norfolk's son would inherit the title: More is advising him to think ahead.
	immutable	unchanging.
72	**Sermon on the Mount**	Christ's sermon on mankind and its nature.
	Thomas Aquinas	a religious philosopher, renowned for the detail of his thought.
73	**a new Act**	the Act of Succession which declared that children borne by Anne Boleyn would become Henry's heirs.

74	**a rack**	an instrument of torture: the victim was tied on the rack by the limbs and stretched.
75	**Thomas Cranmer**	appointed by Henry as Archbishop of Canterbury.
78	**material**	relevant and bearing upon the case under trial.
80	**the Lieutenant**	the governor of the Tower of London.
84	**Eve run out of apples**	More refers to Eve's temptation of Adam.
89	**Foreman of the Jury**	the spokesman of the jury that will decide upon More's guilt or innocence.
	Hall of Westminster	a hall in the ancient palace of Westminster used for state trials.
91	**the Kingdom**	the Kingdom of God, i.e. Heaven.
	betoken	mean.
	His Grace's Title	King Henry's title of Head of the Church of England.
95	**The red dragon**	the heraldic symbol for Wales.
96	**Magna Carta**	The Great Charter, signed by King John in 1215, guaranteed the Church freedom from interference by the monarch, as well as the civil liberties of the English.
	Coronation Oath	On coronation, the new monarch swears to protect the freedom of the Church.
98	**my master**	Jesus Christ.
	easel and gall	according to the Bible, before Christ died on the cross, he was given easel and gall to drink, a bitter, repellent drink.
101	**Alternative ending**	created to define the message or moral more clearly for the benefit of the audience.

BIBLIOGRAPHY

Harold Hobson, (ed.) *Penguin New English Dramatists 6,* Penguin, 1963

Ronald Hayman, *Robert Bolt*, Heinemann, 1969

Ronald Hayman, *British Theatre since 1955*, Oxford University Press, 1979

John Russell Brown, *A Short Guide to Modern British Drama*, Heinemann, 1982

Benedict Nightingale, *An Introduction to 50 Modern British Plays*, Pan, 1982

Gareth Lloyd Evans, (ed.) *Plays in Review, 1956-1980*, Batsford, 1985

In addition, historical accounts of the events of the play can be found in texts covering the Tudor period. The most authoritative biography of Sir Thomas More is:

R. W. Chambers, *Thomas More*, Cape, 1935

Finally, the Author's Preface, at the beginning of this book, contains a detailed account by Robert Bolt of how he sought to use the historical events to dramatize his concerns.